How to crea for the Web using HTML

Other Titles of Interest

How to create pages

for the Web

using HTML

by

John Shelley

BERNARD BABANI (publishing) LTD
THE GRAMPIANS
SHEPHERDS BUSH ROAD
LONDON W6 7NF
ENGLAND

PLEASE NOTE

Although every care has been taken with the production of this book to ensure that any projects, designs, modifications and/or programs, etc., contained herewith, operate in a correct and safe manner and also that any components specified are normally available in Great Britain, the Publishers do not accept responsibility in any way for the failure, including fault in design, of any project, design, modification or program to work correctly or to cause damage to any other equipment that it may be connected to or used in conjunction with, or in respect of any other damage or injury that may be so caused, nor do the Publishers accept responsibility in any way for the failure to obtain specified components.

Notice is also given that if equipment that is still under warranty is modified in any way or used or connected with home-built equipment then that warranty may be void.

First Published – October 1996
Revised and reprinted – February 1998
Reprinted – February 1999

British Library Cataloguing in Publication Data:
A catalogue record for this book is available from the British Library

ISBN 0 85934 404 5

Cover Design by Gregor Arthur
Cover illustration by Adam Willis
Printed and bound in Great Britain by Cox & Wyman Ltd, Reading

Preface

The Internet is the physical means by which information is transmitted from one local area network (LAN) site to another. It consists of wires from office computers to their local network computers (servers), routers which route information from one local network to another via the telephone system, cables and satellites, as well as a set of rules (protocols) for the actual transmission of data agreed by all LANs using the Internet. It is the ultimate example of a Wide Area Network (WAN). See *Other Titles of Interest* for reference texts.

At many of the local networks, information has been stored over the past decade on a vast range of topics in the form of databases, documents, programs, organisations' profiles, sound, film, video and images, etc. The entire collection of all this information stored on these local sites all over the world is called the World Wide Web (WWW). To find and display any of this information on your own home/office computer screen a Web browser program is required. Mosaic, Internet Explorer, Netscape are some examples of such browsers.

Of course, we need to tell the program browser what we want to look for (via a *search program* such as YAHOO or Magellan, two amongst many) or to provide the browser with the name and address of a document (a *URL*, see page 45) given that we know exactly where it is held.

People who create pages of Web information have to tell the browser exactly how the information is to display on a screen: large typeface headings, this phrase to be in bold or italic for emphasis, the following phrases to be listed with bullets or numbers, insert an image here, etc.

Word processor users have to do the same. The main difference between word processor operators and Web page authors is that the former simply clicks on buttons, icons and pull down menu options. They see the effect of their selections immediately, a change in typeface, size, bullets in a list, and so on.

In the case of Web document authors, they have to use the HTML language rather than click on icons and menus. All current Web browsers are designed to recognise documents which are written in the HTML language. It is the purpose of this text to explain how to use the HTML codes which *markup* a Web document.

A document created by a Web author consists not only of the text itself, but also the formatting codes which tell the browser how to display that text.

The HTML language is really a set of codes which authors insert within their text. For example:

<B>This phrase is to be displayed in bold.</B>

Below is what the author intends to be seen in his/her document. The author cannot see what it will look like until it is displayed by a Web browser on a Web screen, unlike a word processor user who can see the immediate effect of formatting text:

This phrase is to be displayed in bold.

The purpose of this text is to discuss the codes available to the HTML author. Anyone can master the language since it is simple to use and learn. This is one of the reasons why the Web has had such a rapid rise in popularity.

I would like to thank Mari-Elena Shelley for reading this text and for making many helpful comments prior to its publication.

I would also like to thank the Science Museum, London, for permitting me to use their home page for illustration. It is one of the finest examples of such a page that I have yet come across, and all home grown! Also, I acknowledge the School of Oriental and African Studies, London, SOAS, for permission to include their logo in some of the examples.

About the Author

John Shelley took his Masters degree in Computing at Imperial College, London, where he has worked as a lecturer in the Centre for Computing Services for some twenty-five years.

He has been Chief Examiner since 1982 for the Oxford Local Delegacy in Computer Studies for their GCE O-level examinations, Senior Examiner for the SEG GCSE Computer Studies (now both defunct) and, at the time of writing, Chief Examiner for O-level Computer Studies for Overseas candidates. Yes! such an examination still exists beyond these shores.

He has written eleven other books on computing. This is his latest text which he hopes will prove useful to those who want to learn HTML at a human level.

He is married with one daughter and would like to dedicate this book to:

Rosalind & Mari-Elena

Trademarks

Contents

Chapter 5: Attributes

Chapter 6: Creating Hypertext Links

Chapter 7: Putting Images onto Web Pages

Chapter 8: Forms

Chapter 12: Frames in HTML

Appendix A

Appendix B:

Glossary

Index

Chapter 1

Introduction to HTML

What is HTML?

It is a language used by people who wish to create documents which are to be displayed as pages of information on the World Wide Web. In other words, if you want to put some information on the Web, you will need to learn HTML - the *hypertext markup language*.

The scene is changing rapidly with new Web browsers fighting for dominance in the market place. Each has its own unique features. However, at the centre of any Web document lies HTML, certainly for the next few years. All Web browsers are designed to recognise and understand the HTML language, that is, a set of formatting codes which tell the browser how to format and display the text.

In the preceding paragraphs, a number of jargon terms have had to be used. The World Wide Web, sometimes known as WWW, W3 or even W^3, is essentially a *concept*. To appreciate this we need to relate this to the Internet. For some decades now, various academic, research and government computer centres have been compiling information on a vast number of topics and storing it on their local network computers. The Internet is the means by which all these different sites are today interconnected to form an international network - hence Internet. Information held at any site can be shared (accessed) by any other site provided it is connected to the Internet. This *interconnection of information* held in all the sites is known as the Web or WWW.

Finding out where information is stored and being able to display copies of it on your own screen is part of the function of a Web browser. It is a program which realises the *concept* of the WWW, rather like Word 6 or WordPerfect 6.1 or Ami Pro realises the concept of word processing. Netscape, Internet Explorer, Mosaic are examples of Web browsers. They are able to browse around the Web, locating and retrieving information which you the user wish to see.

If you are new to the Internet and the WWW, refer to a companion text[1] *The Internet and World Wide Web explained* for more details.

A Problem

There is a problem however. The various sites use different operating systems which are unable to communicate with each other. One analogy is that of natural languages such as French, English, Japanese. Someone knowing only English cannot communicate with someone speaking only in Japanese. The Internet provides a common tongue which allows all the different operating systems to communicate with each other. Basically it is simply a set of rules for communication. The rules are called a *protocol* - this is the purpose of the IP, the Internet Protocol used by all systems wishing to communicate over the Internet.

When you think about it, the same applies to information on the Web. If I want others to read some

---

[1]   Author, J. Shelley, published by Bernard Babani, 1996, book No. BP403.

information which I have created, it may have to be transferred between different operating systems and then displayed on a Mac, an IBM PC, a Unix workstation, an IBM mainframe or some mini-computer. These different systems, called *platforms*, also require some common tongue in order to know how to transfer information (the ***http*** protocol is the one used for the Web). Once a Web browser has received information, it uses HTML to find out how to display that information.

Hypertext Markup Language - HTML

HTML is a simple hypertext markup language. The term *markup* merely refers to the codes used to tell the Web browser how the text is to be displayed, for example, **bold**, *italic,* the size of characters, whether it should be proportional[2] or `monospaced`. The language is the set of codes, called *tags*, used in HTML and that is what this text explains - how to insert codes in basic text and what codes are available. We shall move on to this shortly.

The term *hypertext* requires more explanation.

Hypertext

Imagine you are in a library, searching a card index system for a particular book. When you find the card it will contain details such as the book title, shelf position, author, publisher, date of publication, etc. Now suppose that you would like to know more about the author. Let us say that you could simply point to the author's name on the card and up pops another card with details about the author, including a photograph and details about other books he or she has written. One of these titles interests you and again you point to the title. Lo and behold!

---

[2] See Glossary for terms *proportional* and *monospaced*.

another card pops up from 'nowhere' with a brief summary of the book, cost, shelf position, and so on. You may now wish to go back to the original card, point to the phrase 'shelf position', and a map of the library pops up showing you where the physical shelf is situated. That is what hypertext is all about.

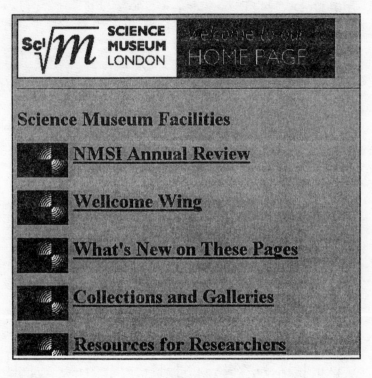

Figure 1.1
Science Museum Home Page

When viewing the WWW, some of the text is in colour, typically blue and frequently underlined as well. This is the actual hypertext itself. See Figure 1.1. The rest of the text is usually black. When the mouse pointer is moved to a piece of hypertext (or indeed a hypertext image) the arrow changes to a hand with a pointing finger. By clicking on the coloured text or image, another page of information appears providing more detail about that text or picture. In turn, this page may have yet other coloured hypertext. By clicking on another hypertext phrase, yet another page of information pops up telling you all about that text. When you have finished, you can click on a button which will take you back to the start - note the Back & Forward buttons at the top in Figure 1.2.

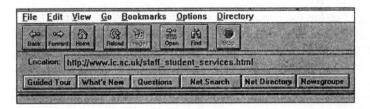

Figure 1.2

It is really quite a simple concept. The coloured text, usually a word or short phrase, or even a picture, has a link to another document which provides more detail about that word or phrase or image. That other document is often simply a separate file, stored on the network's discs, (see Figure 6.1 - Chapter 6) but it could equally well be at any other site in the Internet.

The hypertext phrase has an address to the site and the directory in which the document is held. When you click on the hypertext word, the system is set up to search for that document and to display a copy of it on the screen. The link, called a *hyperlink,* is really an address where the document is stored. It is rather like someone using Windows or the Mac operating system to *open* a file, which has been previously stored on their computer's hard disc. For example:

```
C:\MYDOCS\docname.doc
```

The link includes the site address, the directory (folder) and the name of the file. We shall see how hyperlinks are created in Chapter 6.

It is now time to explain something about the history of HTML.

The Birth of HTML

HTML has been in use by the WWW since 1990. Technically, an HTML document is an example or *instance* of another language, the Standard Generalised Markup Language (SGML). This language originated as a General Markup Language (GML) devised by IBM in the 1960s as an attempt to solve the problem of transferring documents across different computer systems.

Markup is a publishing term referring to the typesetting instructions put in by editors telling the human printers how to layout the manuscript. GML was adopted as a standard by the International Standards Organisation[3] and became known as SGML.

Currently, there are several versions of HTML formally known as *standardisation levels*. Each new level includes certain features unknown to the previous ones.

---

[3] Reference number: ISO 8879:1986.

- Level 0 is the basic, early level, essentially able to display text in a simple manner.

- Level 1 added the ability to include images. All WWW browsers must adhere to level 1.

- Level 2 includes all elements of level 1 plus the ability to allow users to input data, say, for order forms.

- Level 3, often called HTML+, includes tags for objects such as tables, mathematical equations and figures.

Level 1 was a simple markup language to learn and use; and all browsers implemented its features. It was the very simplicity of level 1 that led to the popularity of HTML. Since then certain software manufacturers have been tinkering away, adding non-standard features in the hope that their software would become adopted by most users. It has led to a great deal of uncertainty, but such is life. This book concentrates on level 2 since most Web browsers implement the majority of its features and should still do so for some time to come. In Appendix A, you can find a list of sources from which formal definitions of the various levels can be obtained.

For those who want a full description of the level 2 HTML standard, it can be found in:

```
ftp://ds.internic.net/rfc/rfc1866.txt
```

This refers to the RFC 1866 specification, where RFC stands for Requests for Comments. This standard, usually known as HTML Version 2, has been drawn up by the Network Working Group which is part of the Internet Engineering Task Force, IETF. This text adheres to this standard and when referred to we shall call it RFC 1866.

Included in the text are two features which are not HTML version 2. They are *Tables* and *Frames*. What is covered in Tables has become a virtual standard and can be safely used. Some older browsers, fast disappearing, will not support the table feature, and we have provided a mechanism for coping with the situation.

As for Frames, many current browsers support this feature. Ample warning is given in Chapter 12 about the current battle between the two main browser companies, Microsoft and Netscape so that you will be able to take the necessary precautions when using the frames feature.

Chapter 2

The HTML Language

Basic Elements of HTML

HTML is not a programming language. It is more akin to a *text formatter* which pre-dated word processors. The user had to type in formatting codes as well as the actual text itself. The codes informed the physical printer how to print the text.

HTML consists of two basic elements: *character entities* and *markup tags*. The markup tags are also called *elements* in many reference texts. We shall use both terms in this text. Since we shall not use character entities until Chapter 5, we shall not discuss them here.

Markup Tags

Markup tags are used to describe how a Web browser should present the display of text. Each tag is enclosed in angle brackets - < >. Thus: <B> Bold this text. </B> would result in a Web browser displaying:

Bold this text.

Some tags have two parts, a start tag and an end tag. The ending tag is the same as the starting tag except that it includes a forward slash - /. Everything between the pair of tags will be bold, italic or whatever, usually in Times New Roman. For example:

<I>This text is in italic. </I>
---

would be displayed by a Web browser as:

This text is in italic.

Other tags have just one part, for example: <BR> and <HR>. The former indicates that the *following* text must begin on a new line. <HR> causes a horizontal rule (line) to appear across the screen. These elements are called *empty tags* whilst those which require a pair of tags are called *non-empty tags*.

What goes in between the angle brackets is known as the tag ID - the identification name. The tag name may be in uppercase, lowercase or a mixture: Thus: <hR> <HR> and <hr> are all valid forms of the ID. However, it is *not* correct to put spaces between the brackets or between the letters. Thus: < HR> or < H R > would not be recognised by many Web browsers.

Structure of an HTML Document

An HTML document has two parts, a *head* and a *body*. The **head** contains general information about the document, mainly for the benefit of the browser, and is enclosed in the non-empty pair <HEAD> ... </HEAD>. What is contained in the <HEAD> is not displayed on the screen. Material to be displayed is found within the <BODY> section. For the moment we will use the head section to put in a title.

Although it is not necessary, many browsers use the text within the <TITLE> tag to label the *display window* i.e. the window in which the document is displayed. Also, some Web searcher programs will collect Web document titles and add them to a database[1]. These databases are used by Web programs to search for documents which relate to certain topics. Therefore, the text of the title should be short but sufficient to identify the document's content by use of keywords.

```
<HTML>
<HEAD>
<TITLE>A Title: keyword 1 and keyword 2.</TITLE>
</HEAD>

<BODY>
Text and any images you want displayed....
</BODY>
</HTML>
```

RFC 1866 specifies that all HTML documents must contain a <TITLE> and recommends that the text be less than 64 characters.

The body part, enclosed between the pair <BODY> ... </BODY>, contains the actual text of the document. Blank lines may be included in the source document to make it more readable but they will not affect the display of the document. Strictly speaking, the entire document should be enclosed in <HTML> .. </HTML> tags but is currently optional. We shall not always include them for the sake of brevity.

Let us now create a simple Web document. You may use any text editor or word processor to type the source document which includes both the text and tags but the resulting file must be saved as a *text only* file. In the examples, I used Word 6 for Windows. See

---

[1] See Chapter 10 for more details.

Chapter 11 for more details about using a word processor to create HTML source documents.

Call up your word processor and type in the following source code. Save the file as *text only*. Then use your Web browser to see what the document will look like on the Web. In Netscape, this meant choosing File, then Open File and clicking on the name of the file.

```
<HEAD>
<TITLE>A Simple Example </TITLE>
</HEAD>

<BODY>
<HR>
<H1>Simple Example 1</H1>
<HR>
This is my first exercise. The following text is
<B>bold</B> and <I> italic </I>.
Although this sentence appears on a new line in the
source code, it will be the Web browser which decides
where it will be placed.
</BODY>
```

Simple Example 1

This is my first exercise. The following text is **bold** and *italic*. Although this sentence appears on a new line in the source code, it will be the Web browser which decides where it will be placed.

Notes: Note the use of the empty <HR> tag to create lines before and after the heading - Simple Example 1. The actual heading text is enclosed in a pair of level 1 heading tags - <H1>...</H1>. Headings are discussed below.

Exactly how lines of text are displayed depends upon the browser and the size of the display window which a user has chosen. Browsers ignore extra spaces, tabs and new lines created by pressing the Enter key in the source text. The actual markup tags will obviously not be displayed either. Consequently, it will decide how many words it can display on a line in its window. If you want to force text to begin on a new line then you will have to use the line break <BR> tag or the paragraph tag <P>. See Chapter 4 for details.

We shall next look at *Headings*, but before we do so, it is necessary to understand that each browser displays the HTML tags according to the rules laid down by RFC 1866 and according to any limitations the machine or browser has. Some systems may have only one typeface to use, in which case the browser's ability to differentiate between style tags will be severely limited.

Some of the more recent browsers have access to a range of typefaces and colours and even the ability to blink text.[2] It will decide how each style tag will be displayed. One may be in yellow, another may be in a blinking purple. Such browsers then have a wider choice of how different tags may be displayed. This

---

[2] Some readers find this somewhat distracting, if not distinctly irritating.

should become clearer when we discuss the types of tags available to HTML authors.

Headings - H1 to H6

Note the <H1> tag used in the *Simple Example 1* code above. This denotes a Header 1 level. All text between the starting tag <H1> and the closing tag </H1> will be in large, bold characters. There are six levels in all. Figure 2.1 shows examples of these. Note that some headings are in bold and others in italic. Usually, the text is in Times New Roman and a typical point size is also given. According to RFC 1866, <H2> is displayed less prominently than <H1> but more prominently than <H3>, etc. Actual point sizes and typefaces are not defined and depend upon the browser in use.

Headings have a pre-defined space to separate the heading from the text which follows. Usually this is a 12-point line break *before* and *after* the heading for levels 1 to 4. Levels 5 & 6 have a break after the heading but not before.

You may think that these headings are not very exciting and you are not alone in that thought, but that is all the level 2 HTML will offer. Later versions offer some variation but you should be aware that there are many different browsers and computers in use by people who may chance upon a Web page. On your browser a document may look very fancy but on some others which can only display simple HTML tags the page may look feeble.

Browsers are normally designed to ignore any tags which they cannot recognise either because the author mis-typed them or because the browsers cannot perform the format.

Finally, RFC 1866 recommends that heading levels should be used in order. That is, do not jump from H1 to H3, rather use H1, H2, H3, etc. However, I have yet to come across a browser which enforces this.

Level 1 Heading	18 pt	`<H1>Level 1 Heading</H1>`
Level 2 Heading	16 pt	`<H2>Level 2 Heading</H2>`
Level 3 Heading	14 pt	`<H3>Level 3 Heading</H3>`
Level 4 Heading	12 pt	`<H4>Level 4 Heading</H4>`
Level 5 Heading	11 pt	`<H5>Level 5 Heading</H5>`
Level 6 Heading	10 pt	`<H6>Level 6 Heading</H6>`

Figure 2.1: Levels of Headings
Actual size - typically in Times New Roman and point sizes as shown.

Chapter 3

Formatting Tags

In this chapter, we shall look at those HTML tags which allow text to be formatted in various ways. <B> and <I> are two simple formatting tags. There are some more. All of them are sets of non-empty tags. We shall look at ten and divide them into the following groups:

- Bold: `<B>` & `<STRONG>`
- Italic: `<I>` `<EM>` & `<CITE>`
- Monospaced fonts: `<TT>` `<CODE>` `<KBD>` & `<SAMP>`
- Underlined: `<U>`

<B> & <STRONG>

```
<B> Text between BOLD tags.</B>
<STRONG> Text within STRONG tags.</STRONG>
```

Text between BOLD tags.
Text within STRONG tags.

So what is the difference? Usually no difference at all. Does that mean that I can use either tag and mix them up as demonstrated in the following?

```
The following is
<STRONG>a STRONG phrase</STRONG>
 and this is another phrase in bold
<B>and in the same sentence.</B>
```

> The following is **a STRONG phrase** and this is another phrase in bold **and in the same sentence.**

This is not to be recommended. Text tagged with bold <B> should be displayed in bold by the browser. Text in <STRONG> may also appear in bold, but some of the newer browsers may decide to put <STRONG> text in purple. This would make the sentence above inconsistent. You as the author might well assume that both phrases would be consistently bold but on some browsers the first phrase may be in purple and the second phrase in bold.

The professional HTML author always remembers that there are many different browsers in use. To maintain consistency, the professional would ensure that both phrases are either tagged with <B> or with <STRONG>. Now, no matter what browser is used, both phrases will be displayed in the same way. Some browsers may not have a bold font at all. It will have to decide how to distinguish, if at all, <B> from <STRONG>.

<I> <EM> & <CITE>

According to RFC 1866, <B> text must be rendered (displayed) as distinct from <I> text. So if a browser has not a bold font, then it will have to distinguish between the two in some other manner, or make no distinction at all. This apparent anomaly applies to the other styles which we meet next. Remember that any page you want to put on the Web could be read by one of many different types of browsers.

> <I> Text will be in italics.</I>
> <EM> Text will be emphasised.</EM>

<CITE> Text which refers to a citation.</CITE>

In most cases, all three would be rendered in italic and there would be no difference between them when displayed on the screen. But, there are some browsers out there which may well use different colours to distinguish between <EM> and <CITE> whereas <I> may well be the usual italic font. Some browsers may be designed to flash (blink) a <CITE> text. Imagine the resulting horror if an author marked up text as follows:

There are three main parts to this object:
<I>the first part</I> followed by
<EM>a second part</EM>, and finally
<CITE> the third part.</CITE>

Clearly, the author intends all three phrases to have the same format. This will be the case with many browsers. But imagine a new and fancy browser which would display <I> in normal italic, the <EM> in yellow and the <CITE> in a blinking green! Your sentence which you are publishing for the whole world to read would look very odd on the fancy browser giving the reader a poor impression of its author.[1]

According to RFC 1866, <STRONG> will usually be rendered in bold and must be distinguishable from <EM> which is typically displayed in italics. All it says about <B> and <I> is that <B> indicates bold text. Where a bold font is not available, an alternative representation may be used. <I> indicates italic text. Where an italic font is not available, an alternative

---

[1] Some browsers would not blink text unless a BLINK tag had been used, in which case the document author would be aware of any possible inconsistency.

19

representation may be used. These are the rules a browser designer is confined to if he or she wishes the browser to conform to the RFC 1866 standard. As for <CITE>, it states that it is used to indicate the title of a book or some other citation and is usually displayed in italic. A browser designer can now decide how any of these should be rendered on the screen provided the rendering adheres to the basic rules above.

Thus, if colours and different typefaces and blinks are available, the designer can have a field day. The designer will assume that the HTML author is professional enough to keep a document consistent. Namely, that all citations will be tagged by <CITE>; that <B> and <STRONG> will not be interchanged on a whim, etc. *Buyer Beware and let HTML Authors Beware!*

Monospaced Fonts

There are four 'different' types of *monospaced* fonts, that is a font reminiscent of the erstwhile typewriter, where each character has the same amount of space - e.g.: 'width', whereas this 'width' is in a *proportional* font where each character is given its required amount of space depending on its shape.

<TT>Text is in teletype font.</TT> Where a monospaced font is unavailable, an alternative representation may be used.

<CODE>Text which usually represents computer code.</CODE> It is intended for *short* words or phrases. It is recommended that <PRE> (see page 34) is used when there are multiple lines of code.

<KBD>Text which indicates what a user should type in.</KBD> This is commonly used in instructional manuals where a user is invited to type in some text at the keyboard. It is intended to be distinguishable from <CODE> so that what a user types in (input) is seen to be different from what a computer responds with (output). In most instances, browsers use the same font.

<SAMP>A sequence of literal characters.</SAMP> Text which should not change. It has a nice and precise meaning for computer programmers.

One of the problems when beginning to learn HTML is the variety of tags which effectively end up looking the same. This is probably most true of the monospaced fonts as seen from the following using Netscape version 0.94. All four tags had exactly the same effect.

```
<TT> Text is in teletype font.
<CODE> Text which usually represents computer code.
<KBD> Text which indicates what a user should type in.
<SAMP> A sequence of literal characters.
```

In practice, many old hands at writing HTML documents use one or two of the above four tags (a sub-set). They keep to this sub-set and ignore the rest. For example, many would use <TT> and/or <CODE>, consistently of course, and never use the other two. But we do need to know what the others signify just in case we come across them in someone else's source document.

The source document is what the author types, that is the tags and the text. In Netscape, you can click on View and Source and look at the actual source document which is displayed as a Web page. This is one way of becoming more familiar with HTML.

```
<U> ... </U>
```

This is the underline tag which underlines the enclosed text. However, it was an early Version 2 proposal and is not part of RFC 1866. Many browsers will display such text in italic. Not having underlining is probably a good thing! Typographers, those concerned with the art and appearance of printed matter, regard the use of underlining as distinctly *naff* - crude. I agree whole-heartedly with them since the appearance of the under-line detracts from the clear reading of the text itself.[2] The whole purpose of providing written information is that is should be easy to read. However, there are many who love to underline and they are entitled to do so if they wish. To those we must point out that not all browsers will underline text within <U> tags.

Having looked at most of the markup or formatting tags, it is time to turn our attention to those tags which put *structure* into a document.

---

[2] Hypertext is underlined for the benefit of simple browsers. It is their only means of being able to distinguish normal text from hypertext.

Chapter 4

Structure

When creating an HTML document, the text and any image references are typed along with their various tags. This is totally different to someone creating a page of text using a word processor. With the latter, you merely type the text and tell the word processor to make words bold, change the typeface and size of text, etc. Word wrap is used so that you keep on typing and the word processor will automatically work out when to put the next word on a new line - wrapping text around the right margin.

A word processor automatically inserts codes for bolding, italicising, change of font, blank lines, etc., but the typist does not see them.[1] HTML is not like this. When you press the Enter key to move to the next line, this will not cause a new line to appear on the Web screen.[2] One reason for this is that it must be the browser which has to decide how many words to display on a line. It is the user who chooses the size of the display window for the Web page and the browser has to adjust the text to that particular size.

If you want some text to start on a new line, for example when typing an address, then you must put in a tag to say so. This is the
 - break tag.

---

[1] In WordPerfect such codes can be seen using that wonderful feature 'Reveal Codes'.
[2] But Microsoft Internet Assistant does! It inserts a paragraph break.

23

Thus:

```
<H1>Heading Level 1</H1>John Shelley<BR>
e-mail:j.shelley@ic.ac.uk<BR>
12th Dec 1996
```

would be displayed as:

Heading Level 1

John Shelley
e-mail: j.shelley@ic.ac.uk
12th Dec 1996

Note: There was no need to put a <BR> tag before "John Shelley" since heading levels 1 - 4 have their own line breaks before and after the heading.

There are various tags which allow HTML authors to structure their documents. These are line breaks and paragraph tags, bulleted, indented lists, and a few extra ones.

Line Breaks & Paragraphs -
 & <P>

You need to be aware that browsers ignore *extra* spaces and any line breaks you may put in through your word processor. In other words, the source which you create with your word processor is *not* how the document will look. That is why you have to specify any line breaks through HTML tags. This is not as bad as it may at first appear. For example, spaces are not allowed in tags but when typing you may inadvertently put some in. Fortunately, these "errors" are ignored by most browsers. They will not display the faulty tag nor will they act on it. Thus if I typed:

```
< H3>Heading < /H3>
```

all that some browsers would display is:

```
Heading
```

However, some browsers unable to recognise the faulty </H3> end tag may render the rest of the text in <H3> format since this is the tag which is still in effect.

The <BR> tag causes whatever text *follows* the tag to begin on the next line. Thus:

```
Here is some text. <BR> This text will begin on the
next line.
```

would produce:

```
Here is some text.
This text will begin on the next line.
```

Extra <BR> tags will give additional line spacing. The <BR> tag is an example of an empty tag, that is it has no corresponding end tag.

The paragraph tag <P> causes the text which *follows* to begin as a new paragraph on a new line. The main difference between these two tags is that most browsers insert extra spacing before the paragraph. In addition, and depending on the browser in use, the paragraph may or may not be indented. The <BR> tag will simply put following text on the next line. The <P> tag has an associated end tag - </P>. The end tag is optional. It is frequently included by professionals to make their source code more readable. For the sake of brevity, it is frequently omitted in our examples.

Address & Blockquote

The <ADDRESS> tag is used for addresses, signatures, authorship, etc., and is often placed at the start or end of the body of the document. Typically, the text is in italic and may be indented. The <BR> tag must be used to put following text on separate lines.

The <BLOCKQUOTE> element is used to contain text quoted from another source. A typical rendering may provide a slight left and right indenting and/or italics. It typically provides space above and below the quote.

Browsers with only one font, may put the greater than symbol (>), or some other character, in the left margin of each line of the quotation. (Many e-mail programs do the same when replying to or forwarding mail so that the recipient can distinguish between the reply and the original message.) As with the <ADDRESS> element, the <BR> tag must be used to force any following text to appear on separate lines.

```
<HEAD>
<TITLE> Address & BlockQuote </TITLE>
</HEAD>

<BODY>
The following quotation is taken from Shakespeare:
<BLOCKQUOTE>There is a tide in the affairs of men,
<BR>
Which taken at full flood, leads on to fortune;<BR>
Omitted, all the voyage of their life is drowned <BR>
in shallows and in miseries.
</BLOCKQUOTE>
Brutus, Julius Caesar Act IV Sc. III
<P>
Please address any comments to:
```

```
<P>
<ADDRESS>John Shelley<BR>
e-mail: j.shelley@ic.ac.uk<BR>
12th Dec. 1996<BR>
</P> </ADDRESS>
</BODY>
```

The following quotation is taken from Shakespeare:

> There is a tide in the affairs of men,
> Which taken at full flood, leads on to fortune;
> Omitted, all the voyage of their life is drowned
> in shallows and in miseries.

Brutus, Julius Caesar Act IV Sc. III

Please address any comments to:

John Shelley
e-mail: j.shelley@ic.ac.uk
12th Dec. 1996

Lists

There are several tags which can be used to create lists with bullets <UL>, numbers <OL> and hanging indents <DL>. With the exception of the hanging indent, all the others take the empty list item tag, <LI>, to mark the start of each item in the list.

<UL> ... </UL>
This is the unordered list consisting of a series of short lines, each marked with the <LI> element. Each line is usually marked by a bullet or similar symbol and the

text is indented from the symbol. If text wraps to the next line, it is aligned with the indent.

<DIR> ... </DIR>

This is similar to the <UL>, so similar that it is rendered identically to <UL>, or not implemented at all! RFC 1866 recommends that the list of items should not be more than 20 characters each. Again, each list item is marked with the empty <LI> element. Some browsers may even arrange the items into columns.

```
<HEAD>
<TITLE> Lists </TITLE>
</HEAD>

<BODY>
<H1>UL </H1>
Here is an unordered list, note the bullets:<BR>
<UL>
 <LI>List item 1
 <LI>List item 2. Let's see what happens when this list
item flows over to another line.
 <LI>List item 3
</UL>
<P>
Here is a Directory listing:
<DIR>
 <LI>Column A <LI>Column B
 <LI>Fred <LI>$23.89
 <LI>Mary <LI>$56.89
</DIR>
<P> </BODY>
```

Do not include a space between the <LI> tag and the actual text. If you do, the space will count as part of the text making the list look ragged at the left.

28

Unhappily, in the example below, the <DIR> was no different to a <UL> when using Netscape Version 2.0, but with the Internet Assistant columns were displayed, though not as intended. Even inserting <BR> tags did not produce the desired effect. Use the <PRE> for correct alignment of columns (see below). So perhaps <DIR> is best forgotten.

UL

Here is an unordered list, note the bullets:

- List item 1
- List item 2. Let's see what happens when this list item flows over to another line.
- List item 3

Here is a Directory listing:

- Column A
- Column B
- Fred
- $23.89
- Mary
- $56.89

The above shows the result from Netscape. Below is the result from Internet Assistant.

Here is a Directory listing:

Column A	Column B	Fred
$23.89	Mary	$56.89

Figure 4.1

<MENU> ... </MENU>

This tag is meant to display the items in the menu in a more compact (smaller) fashion than <UL> and may or may not be marked by bullets or similar symbols. It is intended to contain short lines. Each list item is marked with the empty <LI> element. Frequently, however, some browsers make no distinction between <MENU> and <UL>.

Here is an example of the <MENU> tag:

```
<HEAD>
<TITLE> Menu Example</TITLE>
</HEAD>

<BODY>
<H3>MENU</H3>
<P>
<MENU>
  <LI>List item 1
  <LI>List item 2. Let's see what happens when this list
item flows over to another line.
  <LI>List item 3
</MENU>
</BODY>
```

The above code was displayed by several browsers as though the <UL> tag had been used. Since there is often no difference between the three, it may be safer to stay with <UL>.

<OL> ... </OL>

This is similar to <UL> except that list items are numbered. In the following example, note how <OL> and <UL> may be nested to produce a second level of indentation. Each list item is, again, marked with the empty <LI> element.

```
<HEAD>
<TITLE> Lists </TITLE>
</HEAD>

<BODY>
<H3>UL </H3>
Here is an unordered list, note the bullets:<BR>
<UL>
 <LI>List item 1
 <LI>List item 2. Let's see what happens when this list
item flows over to another line.
        <ul>
        <li>substep 1
        <li>substep 2
        </ul>
<LI> List item 3
</UL>
<H3>OL </H3>
Here is an ordered list, note the numbering:<BR>

<OL>
 <LI>List item 1
 <LI>List item 2. Let's see what happens when this list
item flows over to another line.
        <ol>
        <li>substep 1
        <li>substep 2
        </ol>
<LI>List item 3
</OL>
</BODY>
```

Note how the use of indents and change of case helps to make the HTML source document easier to read.

UL

Here is an unordered list, note the bullets:

- List item 1
- List item 2. Let's see what happens when this list item flows over to another line.
    - substep 1
    - substep 2
- List item 3

OL

Here is an ordered list, note the numbering:

1. List item 1
2. List item 2. Let's see what happens when this list item flows over to another line.
    1. substep 1
    2. substep 2
3. List item 3

Note how the <UL> has the same bullet style for the second level. Some browsers may also be able to show a different style for the second level. Again, what will be produced depends on what browser is being used.

The Definition List

<DL> ... </DL>

This is the definition list, effectively used to create hanging lists. It does *not* take the <LI> element, but two other tags, <DT> ... </DT> and its accompanying

<DD> .. </DD>. It is intended for a list of named items (the definition term - <DT>) and an accompanying paragraph of definition or explanation (the <DD>) frequently placed on a new line.

According to RFC 1866, the entire list of items must be enclosed within the <DL> ... </DL> pair. The contents of a <DL> is a sequence of <DT> and <DD> pairs. The <DD> is typically indented after its <DT>.

Most browsers assume the end of a <DT> or <DD> tag when another <DD> or <DT> or the ending definition list tag, </DL>, is encountered. In other words, both </DT> and </DD> are optional. Here is an example:

```
<HEAD>
<TITLE> Exercise for the DLs, DTs and DDs  </TITLE>
</HEAD>
<BODY>
<H2>Glossary</H2>
<DL>
<DT>Def: List <DD>Definition List
<DT>Def: Term <DD> definition term - usually a short
    phrase
<DT>Def: Data <DD> the accompanying definition of the DT
    may extend over several lines if the definition itself be
    lengthy.
</DL></BODY>
```

Glossary

Def: List
        Definition List
Def: Term
        Definition Term - usually a short phrase
Def: Data
        the accompanying definition of the DT may extend
        over several lines if the definition itself be lengthy.

There are two more elements we shall discuss in this chapter. The first is the use of the <PRE> ... </PRE> tag and the second is how to insert comments within an HTML document.

<PRE> ... </PRE>

This is suitable for text which needs to be displayed in a monospaced font. Unlike most other tags, the <PRE> element preserves line breaks and extra spaces. It is ideal for creating columns. According to RFC 1866, horizontal tabs within the text should be equal to 8 space characters, however, it recommends that tabs should *not* be used. It is better to use spaces rather than tabs to maintain consistency. In Figure 4.1, page 29, the <DIR> tag created columns with one browser but not with another. Yet, the columns were not aligned as intended. If we need to create the effect shown in Figure 4.2, then we need to use the <PRE> tag.

```
<HEAD>
<TITLE> PRE tag </TITLE>
</HEAD>

<BODY>
<H2>Use of PRE tag </H2>
Here is some text which has been formatted in a
monospaced font.
<PRE>
Column A            Column B
   Fred                Mary
  £34.56              £45.69
</PRE>
</BODY>
```

> # Use of PRE tag
>
> Here is some text which has been formatted in a monospaced font.
>
> ```
> Column A          Column B
>    Fred             Mary
>   £34.56           £45.69
> ```

Figure 4.2

Text within the <PRE> tags is rendered (displayed) in a fixed-width typewriter font. It is the only mechanism, according to the strict standards of RFC 1866, for displaying tabular data or any other text which requires well-defined columns or relative positions. All other format tags may well display text in a proportional font, even <TT>, <CODE>, <SAMP> and <KBD>.

Any tag which implies some form of structure, such as headings, address, blockquote and lists, must *not* be used within the <PRE> text. Tags which can be used are <B> and <I>. It can also take the anchor tag for hypertext references (see Chapter 6).

Adding Comments

Comments may be added to an HTML document for whatever purpose the author wishes, typically to explain to others what the author is trying to attempt. Comments begin with <!-- and end with --> There must be no space between the exclamation mark '!' and the first --. Otherwise all other spaces are treated as part of the comment. The entire comment is ignored by the browser and is seen only in the source document. Ideally, each comment should begin on a

new line and avoid the use of special characters such as
< >&!, since some older browsers will not interpret them
correctly. See Figure 4.3 for an example of source code
with comments.

We have not mentioned *attributes* in any detail yet, that is
the subject of the next Chapter.

```
<HEAD>
<TITLE> PRE tag </TITLE>
<!-- Date: 5th August, 1997. -->
</HEAD>

<BODY>
<H2>Use of PRE tag </H2>
Here is some text which has been formatted in a
monospaced font.
<!--The February commission rates for Fred and Mary.
It will be displayed in a fixed-width monospaced font. -->
<PRE>
Column A        Column B
   Fred           Mary
 £34.56         £45.69
</PRE>
</BODY>
```

Figure 4.3

Chapter 5

Attributes

Attributes play a major role with some of the tags which have yet to be discussed. However, at this stage we can introduce them in a painless form and be ready to appreciate their usage when we meet some of the more complex attributes.

Not all tags can have *attributes*. We shall examine some attributes for those tags discussed so far. What are attributes? They further define the use of the tag itself and are placed in the starting tag. In a starting tag, spaces and attributes may be allowed between the tag ID and the closing delimiter. They usually take the form of: *attributename = somevalue*

When the attribute's *name* is the same as its *value*, there is no need to include the value. For example, the <DL> tag for lists may take an optional COMPACT attribute as follows:

```
<DL COMPACT="COMPACT"> ... </DL>
```

In the above example, <DL> is the tag ID, COMPACT is the attribute's name and "COMPACT" is the attribute's value asking for a smaller more compact font to be used, if available. Spacing is allowed around the equals symbol. However, since the attribute's name and its value are the same, apart from the quotes, it can be written as: <DL COMPACT>

This attribute is ignored by some browsers. Those that do not ignore it would use a more compact (smaller) font for the enclosed text. Note that the attribute's value is enclosed in double quotes (single quotes are also valid).

The use of the greater than symbol (>) is not permitted in an attribute's value since it is reserved in HTML to mark the end of a tag.[1] Note also the space after the tag identification name - DL. If more than one attribute is permitted, each is separated by a space, *not* a comma.

When using the <PRE> tag an optional WIDTH *attribute* may be used to specify the maximum number of characters per line. This allows some browsers to select a suitable font and indentation. However, some browsers ignore the WIDTH attribute or interpret the number as the *minimum* number of characters the browser should ensure to display on a single line. Version 3 is contemplating the removal of WIDTH altogether! It is probably safer to ignore it as well.

<PRE WIDTH=40> Values of 40, 80 and 132 are recommended for best results.

Some attribute *values* do not require the enclosing quotes. The <PRE> tag's WIDTH attribute is such an example. <PRE WIDTH = 80>. These are technically called *name tokens* and are digits, as is the case here, or letters, periods or hyphens. Name tokens do not require quotes and are not case sensitive. However, it appears that using quotes is always acceptable whereas their absence can cause problems with some browsers.

---

[1] If you need to include a greater than symbol, then character entities are required. See page 39.

The <HR> tag may also take the WIDTH attribute but this is an extension of Netscape and not a general implementation. RFC 1866 simply states that a horizontal rule is typically full width. Some browsers may present a more imaginative style and a slight left and right indent. Where possible, avoid attributes which may lead to inconsistency. Some attributes are specifically defined by the RFC 1866 standard, and we shall draw attention to these as they appear. Some additional and standard attributes are being proposed for Version 3. We shall refer only to those attributes specified by Version 2 and according to the RFC 1866 standard.

List tags, namely, <UL>, <OL>, <DIR> and <DL>, may take the COMPACT attribute.

If you recall, the <MENU> element is typically rendered, according to RFC 1866, in a compact manner, that means a smaller font. It is not implemented by some browsers. Since <UL> has the COMPACT attribute and bullets, many authors ignore the <MENU> and achieve the same effect by its use with <UL COMPACT>. Version 3 proposes to do away with <MENU>, so perhaps you should begin to ignore it as well!

Character Entities

Some symbols such as the < > " & /, have a particular meaning when typed into HTML source documents. If you need these characters, or other characters such as ½, ¼, to be displayed as part of the text, some browsers would become confused since they would not be able to distinguish between an HTML symbol or the character you wish to display. The answer is to use *character entities.*

For example, should it be necessary to display:

"and <P> indicates the start of a new paragraph."

perhaps as part of a reference manual on HTML, typing <P> as it stands would simply be interpreted as the start of a new paragraph. It, therefore, becomes necessary to use character entities for the *greater than* (>) and *less than* (<) symbols, as follows:

and <P> indicates the start of a new paragraph.

A character entity begins with an ampersand symbol immediately followed by the name of the entity and concludes with a semi-colon. A reference to a complete list of character entity names can be found in Appendix A, but here are some commonly used ones:

Ch. Entity	Meaning	Symbol
<	less than symbol	<
>	greater than	>
"	double quote mark	"
&	ampersand	&
¼	one fourth fraction	¼
½	half fraction	½
¾	three-fourths fraction	¾

The latter three have no names at Version 2, e.g. "gt" for "greater than", although Version 3 is proposing names. However, they do have an ISO 8859-1 number.[2] This number consists of a *hash* sign (#) followed by the decimal number of the character. The hash symbol is sometimes referred to as the *pound* or the *number* sign.

---

[2] See Appendix A for further details.

```
<HEAD>
<TITLE> Character Entities </TITLE>
</HEAD>

<BODY>
Here are two hash symbols:  -- &#35; &#35; <BR>
The pound sterling &#163; <BR>
The word<STRONG>format</STRONG>
is in &lt;STRONG&gt;

</BODY>
```

Here are two hash symbols: -- # #
The pound sterling £
The word **format** is in <STRONG>

Having looked at the basic HTML document, formatting tags, how to structure text and been introduced to attributes and character entities it is now time to move on to creating *hypertext links*.

Chapter 6

Creating Hypertext Links

One of the main reasons for the interest in Web documents is that they can contain *hypertext* as well as ordinary text. Hypertext is usually marked in a special way by Web browsers, typically coloured blue and/or underlined. When moving the mouse pointer over a piece of hypertext a little pointing hand appears rather like that in Windows when in the Help window. By clicking on the hypertext, another document appears. In HTML, the hypertext contains a link address to the other document. It is frequently called a *link* or *hyperlink*.

To create hypertext in HTML the <A> ... </A> tag is used. Whatever is typed between the tags becomes hypertext. The <A> stands for *anchor,* but by itself it is useless, it requires attributes before it will do anything. One of the main attributes is HREF - meaning a *hypertext reference*. This is required to point to where the document to be displayed is kept.

HREF

When a hypertext link is clicked, what is next displayed may be

- a document held on another server *anywhere* in the world
- a document held in the *same directory* as the current document
- or, some other position within the *same document*

43

The latter is useful when a document is long and a user may wish to move to a particular part of the document immediately without having to scroll down. The following example is a single document which has information about the various courses a Centre may offer. The reader can immediately jump to the one he or she is interested in, or find details of how to get to the Centre, how to register, etc., by clicking on the relevant piece of hypertext (underlined in the example).

Training Centre Courses

Venue   -   How to Find Us
How to Register

Courses:

Windows 95
Mac Operating System
Unix Operating System
Word 6 for Windows
WordPerfect 6.1 for Windows
Excel 5 for Windows
Lotus 5 for Windows

Venue

The Training Centre is situated in ..... etc.

Registration Details

To register for a course ..... etc.

Courses

...
...
Windows 95 ... etc.

It is the HREF attribute of the anchor tag which provides the necessary information for the Web browser to find and display the referenced text. Figure 6.1 illustrates this where the documents happen to be stored at the same site, but the documents could be stored at another site anywhere in the world.

Document at a Different Site

To point to documents held at a site other than your own local site, the link must contain a *complete* URL.

URL

A URL consists of:

- the *method* by which a document is accessed
- the name of the *site* (server) where the document is held
- a *port number* to be used on the server - (if required)
- the name of the document - *file name*
- the name of a *section* within a document - preceded by the # symbol (sections are optional)

Example:

http://www.ic.ac.uk:1080/docname.html#section3

`http` is the Web's own method for accessing and transferring documents between different sites. It stands for the *hypertext transfer protocol*. It is a set of rules (the protocol) used by the network servers for transmitting data.

`://` is a separator marking off the transmission protocol from the rest

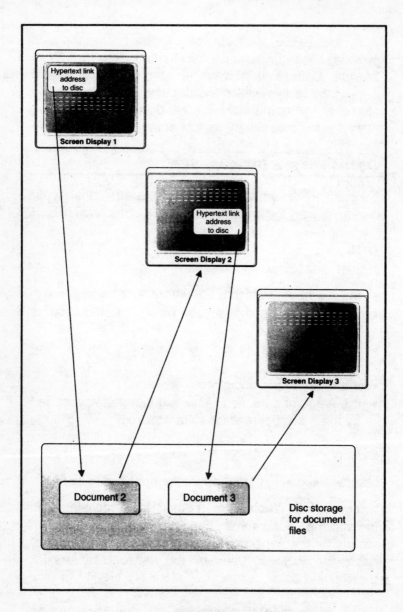

Figure 6.1
Hypertext links to documents stored at the same site

46

`www.ic.ac.uk` is the site address of where the document is stored, here the Web server (www) at Imperial College (ic) which is part of the academic community (ac) in the United Kingdom (uk)

`:1080` here a (fictional) port number used by the Web server; usually not required since a default port number is used, but must be specified if given in a URL

`docname.html` the actual file or document name held in the server's storage discs

`#section3` a reference to a particular section within the document (see NAME below)

```
There is more information in
<A HREF=
"http://www.ic.ac.uk:1080/docname.html#section3">
Section 3</A> for those who are interested.
```

Would appear as:

There is more information in **Section 3** for those who are interested.

Clicking on **Section 3** would cause the browser to find and display whatever `docname.html` has to say at the point marked *section 3*. Furthermore, Section 3 would be displayed at the top of the screen.

Thus, if one was reading a document containing the above HTML code at a site in, say, Houston, Texas, the Web browser would contact the Web server at Imperial College, obtain a copy of `docname.html` and display the document at the point marked *section 3* on the computer screen in Houston, Texas. If the URL did not contain #section3, as illustrated below, then the browser would display the information at the *start* of the document.

```
<A HREF=" http://www.ic.ac.uk:1080/docname.html">
... </A> etc.
```

Document at Same Site

Should a document referenced by some hypertext reside in the same *directory* as the document you are reading, a shorter form can be used. These are called *partial* or *relative* addresses or links.

```
<A HREF="docname.html#section3"> ... </A>
```

The above code will assume that the document pointed to by the HREF attribute is another file in the *same* directory and on the *same* server as the actual document you are looking at.

Should the document be in a sub-directory of the current directory in which the document you are reading is stored, then that sub-directory would have to be included. Thus, if a document referenced by a hyperlink is in a sub-directory named admin, then the following code would be used:

```
<A HREF="admin/docname.html"> ... </A>
```

These are called relative links or addresses simply because the path specified to the other document is relative to the location (directory) of the current file.

Advantages of Using Relative Links

One advantage of using relative links is that it reduces typing and, clearly the risk of mis-typing. But there is another and more important advantage. Use of partial links means that a group of documents can be easily moved to some other location. For example, a group of documents may comprise information about various research projects in a department. These documents could be held in a particular directory on the department's server. Let us suppose that there are references to them in a main document.

Should it become necessary to move the documents to a different site or directory, it will not be necessary to update all the links in the main document. The relative links will become relative to the new location of the main document. Of course, the original URL of the main document will have to be changed so that users can locate its new location. Once they have done so, all links in the main document become relative to its new location.

Within the Same Document

To create a link in a document to some other point within the *same* document, the HREF must contain a pointer to that position and make use of the NAME attribute at that point. Figure 6.2 gives an example and relates to the illustration on page 44.

Clicking on the hypertext 'Venue' will cause the browser to search for the marker `venue` elsewhere in the document and display what is at that point at the top of the window. A click on 'How to Register' would jump to the marked point `H2Reg`. Note the # symbol is required in the HREF immediately followed by the marker, whereas in the NAME attribute only the marker's name is required.

```
<A HREF="#venue">Venue</A> - How to Find Us
<A HREF="#H2Reg">How to Register</A>
.....
.....
<H3><A NAME="venue">Venue</A></H3>
The Training Centre is situated in ..... etc.
...
<H3><A NAME="H2Reg">Registration Details</A>
</H3>
To register for a course .... etc.
...
```

Figure 6.2

Browsers do not display the text in <A> tags with a NAME attribute (the marked point) in any special way. However, it is quite likely that the author may wish to format that text with, say, a level 3 heading. It is important that the pair of <A> tags are contained *within* the format tags. Thus, if 'Registration Details' were formatted as:

<H3>Registration Details</H3>, then the <H3> tags should contain the pair of <A> tags thus:

```
<H3>  <A NAME="H2Reg">Registration Details </A>
</H3>
```

NOT:

```
<A  NAME="H2Reg" ><H3>Registration Details </H3>
</A>
```

<BASE>

The <BASE> tag is used to refer to the absolute URL
to be used for any relative links in a particular
document. It is placed in the <HEAD> of the document,
but I have seen them placed before the <HEAD> and
apparently still work. Not to be recommended!

It is an empty tag and is optional. Therefore, why use
it? If present, BASE has one attribute (mandatory),
namely, HREF. This reference is called the *base* URL
of the document. It contains the *original* location
address of the current document. If this document, for
one reason or another, becomes separated from the
documents referred to by relative links, there is no
need to alter all those relative links or to move all those
documents to where the main document is now stored.

Remember, that if a document is moved away from its
original location, then all relative URLs are no longer
valid. However, if the BASE is present, all relative
URLs in this document are evaluated according to this
base URL and can be correctly located.

```
<HEAD>
<BASE HREF="somesite.edu/dir/sub-dir/file.html">
</HEAD>
```

Other Protocols

http indicates the Web protocol, but many other
protocols can be used as well.

`file:` This method causes the browser to load a file from the locally accessible disc system and is frequently used to preview Web pages being developed on a computer that has a browser but no server. It is possible that `file` may be dropped from newer versions.

`ftp:` file transport protocol.

`mailto:` E-mail Form (see Chapter 8). The e-mail address follows the colon (:).

`news:` USENET news - the group or article name follows the colon.

`gopher:` the gopher protocol used to search for information on the Web.

`telnet:` an earlier Internet tool for accessing resources at another site.

Hypertext & Courtesy

It is customary to enable a user to return to the starting point of a main document. Let us suppose that a user has clicked on a hypertext reference which calls up some other related document anywhere in the world (or, indeed, another part of the same document). Having read the information, the user now wishes to return to the main document (typically a list of contents) in order to visit some other document.

Many HTML authors supply hypertext references, such as 'Return to Contents' which is simply a reference back to the start of the main document. This little courtesy saves the user having to, perhaps several times, click on the browser's Go Back button. Here is an example.

```
<HEAD>
<TITLE> Document A Source code </TITLE> </HEAD>

<BODY>
<H2>Contents List</H2>
<UL>
   <LI><A HREF="intr-org.html">Introduction to
        our Organisation</A>
   <LI><A HREF="staff.html">Staff Members</A>
   <LI><A HREF="pgcrs.html">Post Graduate
        Courses</A>
   <LI> etc.
</UL> </BODY>
```

In Document A - called DOCA.html:

Contents List

- Introduction to our Organisation
- Staff Members
- Post Graduate Courses

```
<HEAD>
<TITLE> Document B Source code</TITLE>
<!-- Post Graduate Courses -->
</HEAD>

<BODY>
<H2>Post Graduate Courses</H2>
<UL> <LI><A HREF="chem_research.html">Chemical
            Research</A>
.......etc.
<A HREF="DOCA.html">Return to Contents List</A>
</BODY>
```

Clicking on 'Post Graduate Courses' in Document A would display Document B. Clicking on 'Return to Contents List' in Document B would force the browser to locate and re-display Document A.

How to do it within a single document:

```
<H2><A NAME="Top">Contents List</A></H2>
......
......
<A HREF="#Top">Return to Top</A>
```

Contents List
....
.... etc.
Return to Top

Clicking on 'Return to Top' would cause the browser to search for the marker 'Top' attached as the value of a NAME attribute within the same document. In other words, it would cause the browser to re-display the same document with the Contents List positioned at the top of the screen.

Chapter 7

Putting Images onto Web Pages

Adding an image or picture can brighten up your Web pages. Most Web browsers can display images as well as text but it should be remembered that each image takes time to process and, therefore, increases the time taken to display the document. Likewise, the bigger the image, the longer it takes. Most Web browsers can display images in X Bitmap (.xbm), GIF (.gif) and JPEG (.jpeg) formats. We have more to say about these formats later.

<IMG>

An image can be:

- inserted by itself anywhere in a document - just for decorative purposes
- inserted along with text
- inserted as a hypertext link so that when clicked it will display information

We shall look at these in order.

Inserting an Image for Decoration

The <IMG> tag has no end tag, that is, it is empty. However, it must contain at least one attribute, SRC (source), telling the browser where to find the image. Images are stored as separate image files. Therefore, a document which incorporates an image must contain not only the image *tag* but also the *location* of where the image file is stored. The SRC is in fact an image equivalent of the HREF attribute and the syntax is identical to that of HREF. Here is an example:

```
<HEAD>
<TITLE>Putting in an image. </TITLE>
<BASE HREF="file://d:\htmlbaba">
</HEAD>

<BODY>
<H1>Text with an Image</H1>
Below is the SOAS logo: School of Oriental and African
Studies, London.<P>
<IMG SRC="soas.gif"> </P>
Other text follows here.
</BODY>
```

Text with an Image

Below is the SOAS logo: School of Oriental and African Studies, London.

Other text follows here.

Note: To ensure the image is separated from any other text in the document the paragraph tag is used. Adding the optional end tag </P> makes it clear that the image is meant to be separated from the text.

To test this code on my local PC, I included a <BASE> reference to:

`D:/htmlbaba` the folder where the image is stored. Note also the use of `file://` to indicate my local disc.

The basic syntax is: <IMG SRC="*URL*"> If the image file is in the same location as the document then *relative* links may be used. If the file is in a sub-directory of the current directory then the sub-directory needs to be included.

```
<IMG SRC="/sub-direct/oddface.gif">
```

Likewise, if the image file is stored elsewhere, then the full URL must be given:

```
<IMG SRC="http://www.ic.ac.uk/images/oddface.gif">
```

To Include Text with an Image

In the above example, the image was displayed in its own 'surrounding', text above and below but it is possible for text to flow on the same line as the image, for example:

 **Where to pitch your tent!**

Most sites provide information about their facilities.

```
<H3><IMG SRC="tent.gif">
Where to pitch your tent!</H3>
Most sites provide information about their facilities.
```

Note how the text is aligned at the bottom of the image
- this is the default position. See ALIGN below for other
placements.

Making an Image a Hypertext-Link

To turn an image into hypertext, we need to include
the IMG tag *within* an anchor tag, <A>, thus:

```
<A HREF="URL">  <IMG SRC="URL">  </A>
```

Note the inclusion of the HREF attribute in the starting
<A> tag, followed by the <IMG> tag with its own URL.
The IMG-url allows for the image to be loaded into the
current document. The HREF-url provides the location
for the HTML document to be displayed when the
image is clicked. This document could be a text file, or,
indeed, another image file.

A slight refinement could include the above image *and*
a piece of hypertext, either of which could be clicked to
display the document referenced by the HREF-url.

```
<A  HREF="URL"><IMG SRC="URL"> or this text</A>
```

If you remove the <IMG> tag from the above, we are
left with a normal piece of hypertext code. Add the
<IMG> tag within the anchor element and we have
made the image as well as the text a hypertext link to
the document referenced in the HREF-url, either of
which could be clicked to obtain the file referenced by
the HREF.

There are two more attributes associated with the
<IMG> tag, the ALT and the ALIGN.

ALT="*text*"

Not everyone has browsers which can display images, although this is becoming rare today. However, in order to speed up display, some browsers allow an option to turn off '*the display of images*' - this is not uncommon especially when people have slow connections. So what do these people see?

They will see whatever text you have typed between the double quotes in the ALT (Alternative) attribute, thus:

```
<IMG SRC="http://www.ic.ac.uk/images/oddface.gif"
ALT="An Odd Face">
```

It is a matter of courtesy to let those in the above situations know what they are missing. So in place of the image, they see your text. (Some graphical browsers actually display this text until the image file is finally loaded into the document.)

ALIGN="*position*"

The position can be top, bottom or middle. It specifies the alignment of the image with the accompanying text. The following shows the results of using all three.

```
<IMG SRC="/images/oddface.gif" ALIGN=Top>
Top Text

<IMG SRC="/images/oddface.gif" ALIGN = Bottom>
Bottom Text

<IMG SRC="/images/oddface.gif" ALIGN = Middle>
Middle Text
```

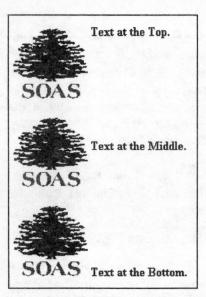

Note that with short phrases the text aligns as desired. However, if the text runs into a sentence, the rest of the text which does not fit on the line will automatically drop to the *bottom* of the image. This means quite a gap between the lines of text. Perhaps the use of bottom (or not to use the ALIGN attribute at all, since bottom is the default) is the best choice.

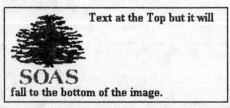

To overcome this problem, Netscape has introduced two new alignments, RIGHT & LEFT to position the image and allow text to wrap the full height of the image. However, it is only supported by that browser as yet.

Image Formats

There are many different formats for storing digital images. Each has advantages and disadvantages. At the present time, Web browsers are able to recognise just a few of these formats. Thus, any image to be inserted in a document should conform to one of these formats.

GIF

The most universally accepted image format on the WWW is the GIF format - Graphics Interchange Format - with a `.gif` filename extension. It is a format which all graphical Web browsers can recognise. It is especially useful if the picture is a small or a graphical image such as logos or icons. It can store black-and-white, greyscale and colour images, although it is limited to 256 colours per image. The image is compressed resulting in a small file which can be displayed quickly on your pages.

The GIF format stores images as a sequence of thin horizontal strips, 1 pixel high. (Figure 7.1 shows the little boxes or *pixels*) This is the reason you can frequently see your image being built up in thin strips. However, GIF images can also be *interlaced*.

In this form the strips are stored in a non-sequential order, say strip 1, 11, 21, 31, 41, etc., followed by strips 2, 12, 22, 32, 42, etc. The advantage of this method is that the image can be displayed as a rough outline which gradually gets filled in with more and more detail. Both methods take about the same time to be completely displayed.

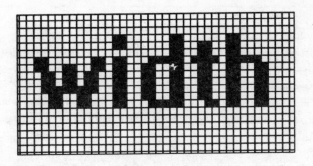

Figure 7.1
Each square box is a pixel

When deciding on using images with a GIF format, it is advisable to be aware that most computers are equipped with graphics cards which can display only 256 colours at one time. Thus, if two GIF images are being displayed, say each with 256 colours (512 in total), simultaneously, there will be problems. In this situation, most browsers, will try to find a set of 256 colours suitable for both images - this practice is known as *dithering*. The end result is often far from satisfactory for either image.

JPEG

JPEG (Joint Photographic Experts Group) is a format especially designed for storing photographic images. Its file extension is `.jpeg` or `.jpg`. Not all browsers support JPEG.

Generally, speaking, JPEG format is better than GIF for photographic images. The quality is better and through its more sophisticated compression techniques the resulting files are smaller than an equivalent GIF file.

X-Pixelmap & X-Bitmap

Two other formats are the X-Pixelmap and its black and white cousin X-Bitmap. Their extensions are `.xpm` and `.xbm` respectively. These do not compress the files and are an inefficient way of storing image files.

X-Bitmaps are a common format on Unix workstations and are frequently found in image and icon libraries. Most browsers treat the white portion of the black and white image as *transparent*. The black part is displayed in black, but whatever background colour (see page 127) is used for the underlying window shows through the white parts. This makes the black image more attractive.

The X-Pixelmap is similar but supports colour. Its main drawback is the size of resulting files.

Portable Network Graphic

The last format we shall mention is the Portable Network Graphic (`.png`). At the present time, it is not widely supported. Like GIF, it allows for transparency, interlacing and image compression. It has better colour quality than GIF and is beginning to be supported by later versions of browsers. Doubtless other formats are in the pipeline.

Loading Images

How are images loaded into a document? The browser first retrieves the document itself and then looks for any <IMG> elements. This entails making further connections to the server holding these image files by using the SRC-url. Thus a document with five images requires six separate connections to the server which clearly involves more time before the complete document and its five images can be displayed. It is the image file extension which enables the browser to decide (if it can) how to process and display the image.

Images may be placed almost anywhere in a document except within the <PRE> tag.

Images which have been scanned using one of the many available scanners are frequently saved in a non-GIF format. However, a number of programs, such as Lview, exist which can be used to open such files and save them in GIF, JPEG, etc., formats, ready to be incorporated into Web documents.

Chapter 8

Forms

HTML provides a means whereby information may be typed into a Web page by a user, collected and sent off to some other location. In other words, you can solicit user input from your Web page readers. Here are some instances where forms may be useful:

- registering for courses
- sending credit card details (!) for ordering goods
- forwarding abstracts of research papers for storage in a database
- forwarding comments about the worthiness of some article to its author
- details for an on-line questionnaire
- soliciting information to be sent to a specific e-mail address
- searching on keywords in a database, etc.

The <FORM> tag is the HTML 2 method for creating fill-in forms within a document. The basic idea is that the user is invited to type information into various areas within the form. These may be blank text areas into which the user types in text, radio buttons, check boxes, pop-up menus (for selecting items from a list) and submit / reset buttons. When the submit button is clicked, the data (user input) is collected together and sent off to its destination. The reset button clears any data entered by the user so that he or she may start again.

There is a problem. Each form sent via the `http` protocol has to have a program specifically designed to process that particular set of data. It is similar to the days when people used computers to solve problems using languages such as Fortran, Cobol, Pascal. If someone wanted to add up three numbers, a program had to be written. If the same person wanted to add up five numbers and find the average *another* program had to be written. So it is with each form on a Web page. In order to write the program to handle the form's data, specific knowledge of the server and the language is required.

These form programs may be written in C, C++ or Pascal; or, scripts (a Unix term for server programs) written in *perl, tcl* or one of the various shell programs such as Bourne. It is beyond the scope of this text to study this area[1] and in any case, creating forms frequently has to be undertaken alongside the Web server staff. However, there is one type of form which does *not* need such detailed knowledge. This is what we shall discuss later in this Chapter.

CGI

The Common Gateway Interface (CGI) is the standard mechanism for communication between http servers and the forms programs, frequently called *gateway programs*. The *gateway program* is the program which processes the data sent from a Web page form. When a Web form is filled in, the user clicks on a submit button. The browser, now called a *client*, sends the data to the server site where the processing program resides. That server will then activate the program and pass it the data. Once the data is processed by the

---

[1] For a full discussion on forms you need to read one of the many specialist texts which discusses the whole area of forms.

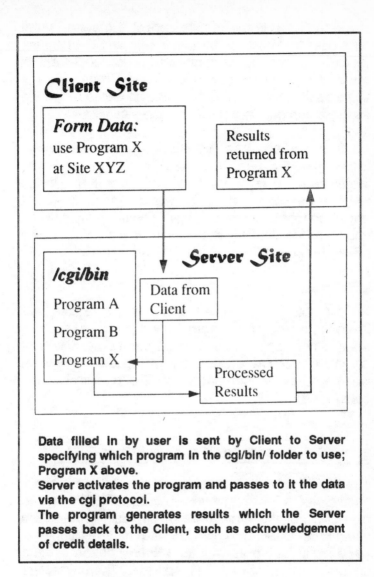

Data filled in by user is sent by Client to Server specifying which program in the cgi/bin/ folder to use; Program X above.

Server activates the program and passes to it the data via the cgi protocol.

The program generates results which the Server passes back to the Client, such as acknowledgement of credit details.

Figure 8.1

program, it sends the results back to the server which then passes it back to the Web client and the user will receive the results, perhaps an acknowledgement of the receipt of some transaction. See Figure 8.1. The CGI specifications define how data is passed from the server to the gateway program, and vice versa.

Each server site has a special directory for storing these gateway programs, usually, /cgi-bin/. As mentioned above, there is one type of form design which bypasses the need for such programs or scripts having to reside on some distant server, namely, when you want the data to be e-mailed *directly* to your own office computer via your local network server.

<FORM>

An example is shown in Fig 8.2 where readers are invited to register for a Word 6 course. It could apply to many other applications such as requesting details of company products or, perhaps, a research document which we have written and would like to solicit readers comments upon it.

How can we construct such a form?

The FORM tag has a starting and an ending tag and it must contain at least two attributes: METHOD and ACTION. For the form to be of any use, it must also contain at least an <INPUT> tag and frequently a <TEXTAREA> tag as well as a *submit* button to send the data off to the e-mail address. There may be several FORMs in a document, but FORMs cannot be nested.

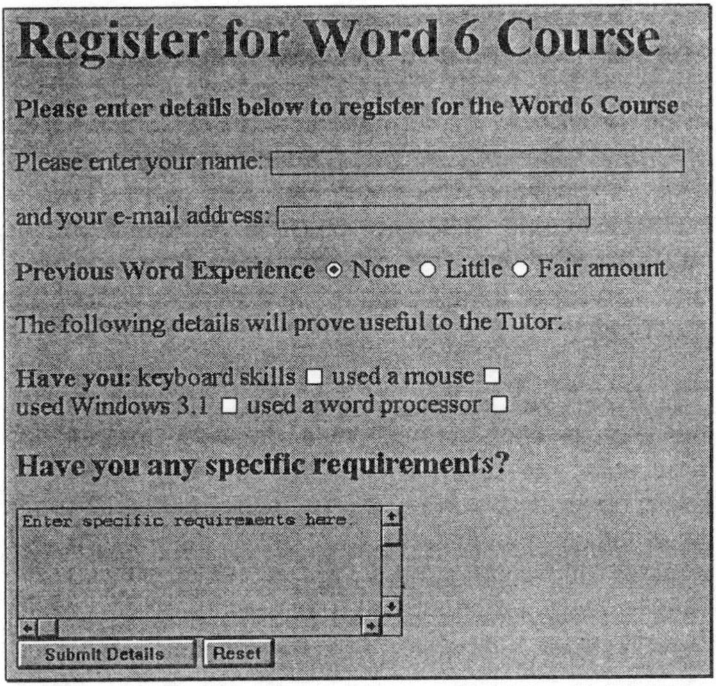

Register for Word 6 Course

Please enter details below to register for the Word 6 Course

Please enter your name: [_____]

and your e-mail address: [_____]

Previous Word Experience ⦿ None ○ Little ○ Fair amount

The following details will prove useful to the Tutor:

Have you: keyboard skills ☐ used a mouse ☐
used Windows 3.1 ☐ used a word processor ☐

Have you any specific requirements?

```
Enter specific requirements here.
```

[Submit Details] [Reset]

Figure 8.2

```
<BODY>
.........
<FORM METHOD=POST
ACTION="mailto:myname@someplace">
<INPUT attributes>
<TEXTAREA attributes> </TEXTAREA>
<INPUT TYPE="submit">
</FORM>
.......
</BODY>
```

METHOD attribute

The METHOD attribute can take one of two values, either GET or POST. The GET appends the data filled in by the user to the form-document's URL. It is called a *query* URL and consists of the form-document's URL, a question mark and the data itself. This is passed to the gateway program specified in an ACTION attribute. That program uses the data to do any number of things such as searching or updating a database.

The POST value, the one we need, determines that the data is sent (posted) to a gateway program for processing, or to an e-mail address. But instead of being appended to the URL, the data is sent as a block to standard input. Note that these values are *not* enclosed in double quotes. GET is the default value.

Exactly what the differences are between GET and POST are beyond the scope of this book and is the subject of specialist texts on forms and gateway programming.

ACTION attribute

When the submit button is clicked, the data typed in by the user will be sent to the URL specified in the ACTION value.[2] For example:

```
<FORM METHOD=POST
ACTION="http://www.abc.edu/cgi-bin/gateprog">

<FORM METHOD=POST
ACTION="mailto:fred@xyz.ac.uk">
```

---

[2] We now have three attributes which take a URL; the HREF, the SRC and here the ACTION.

The first example would send the data to `gateprog` stored in the gateway programs' directory (`/cgi-bin/`) at the Web site `www.abc.edu` for processing via the `cgi` protocol. The `gateprog` program would have to exist. The second example would send the data to the e-mail address referenced in the ACTION attribute, using the `mailto:` protocol. Note the double quotes around each of the URLs.

<INPUT>

This tag allows users to type in information. It is an empty element and requires at least two attributes: TYPE and NAME.

TYPE="display"

The value of the TYPE attribute specifies which type of input mechanism to display in a form. The following lists the various input mechanisms allowed.

"text"	for entry of typed text
"radio"	for the display of a radio button, more than one is required
"checkbox"	for display of checkbox(es)
"submit"	for display of a submit button
"reset"	for display of a reset button
"select"	for display of a menu of options

Examples:

In the following examples, the NAME attribute is required to specify the *variable name* in which data is stored. We shall see how this is used when we look at how the data is actually received at the distant server or by an e-mail program. Remember that a special program, except for an e-mail submission, needs to be

71

designed alongside the HTML document. The program is designed to recognise and process the data held in the variable names chosen by the form's author.

When the TYPE is text, the SIZE attribute simply states the box width. In the following example, a size of 40 characters has been chosen.

```
<INPUT TYPE="text"  NAME="name-person"
SIZE=40>
```

If "Jones" is typed into the 40-character text box it will be associated with the NAME value 'name-person':

```
name-person=Jones
```

When the submit button is clicked, this phrase, along with any other input-data, will be sent to the e-mail address specified in the ACTION attribute of the FORM tag.

In the following example:

```
<INPUT TYPE="radio"  NAME="choice"
VALUE="Good">  Material Good
<INPUT TYPE="radio"  NAME="choice"  VALUE="Not-
good">  Material Poor
```

two radio buttons would be displayed with the text specified after the INPUT tag displayed to the right of the button.

```
O  Material Good    O  Material Poor
```

Normally a series of radio buttons are required, say, when the choice to be made is one from a range such as 'Good, Average, Poor'. Since radio buttons are mutually exclusive, the NAME value ("choice" above) must be the same in each case.

An e-mail program would receive the phrase:

either: `choice=Good` or: `choice=Not-good`

The same format applies to checkboxes, except that the NAME-value in each case must be different since *none* or *all* checkboxes may be selected. In this way, each selection can be stored in a separate variable name. An example is given at the end of this chapter.

```
<INPUT TYPE="checkbox" NAME="discipline"
VALUE="chem"> Chemistry
```

Both radio and checkboxes take an additional attribute, VALUE. Whatever appears in quotes after the VALUE attribute is what is to be associated with the NAME attribute's value. Thus, provided the user checked the box, the above would appear in an e-mail message as:

`discipline=chem`

If all these items of data, including the radio button 'Material Good' were sent to the e-mail address, they would appear as:

```
name-person=Jones&choice=Good&discipline=chem
```

Each *name=value* pair is separated by ampersands (&). This is discussed in more detail below.

```
<INPUT TYPE="submit" VALUE="Send Information">
<INPUT TYPE="reset">
```

In the above, two buttons would be displayed. Clicking the submit button would send off the information to the URL defined in the <FORM> ACTION attribute. Since an optional VALUE attribute has been included, the button would read: 'Send Information' rather than the word *Submit*. The Reset button has no VALUE, in this example, and would simply read as *RESET*. When clicked, it clears all input data entered by the reader.

Finally, there is another text input field which is used when multiple lines of input are requested, such as comments. This is done via the <TEXTAREA> tag, which unlike the INPUT tag, requires a start and an end tag.

```
<TEXTAREA NAME="comment" ROWS=6
COLS = 35>Please enter any comments here.
</TEXTAREA>
```

Here, six rows and 35 columns are displayed, into which the reader can type comments.

Let us now use all this information to code the example shown in Figure 8.2.

```
<HEAD>
<TITLE>Registration for Word 6</TITLE>
</HEAD>

<BODY>
<H1>Register for Word 6 Course</H1>

<P>
<STRONG>Please enter details below to register for the Word 6 Course</STRONG>

<FORM   METHOD=POST
 ACTION="mailto:j.shelley@ic.ac.uk">

<P>
Please enter your name:
<INPUT TYPE="text" NAME="attendee" SIZE=40>

<P>
and your e-mail address:
<INPUT TYPE="text" NAME="mailadd" SIZE=30>
```

74

```html
<P>
<STRONG>Previous Word Experience</STRONG>
<INPUT TYPE="radio" NAME="experience" VALUE="None"
CHECKED> None

<INPUT TYPE="radio" NAME="experience" VALUE="Little">
Little

<INPUT TYPE="radio" NAME="experience"
VALUE="Famount"> Fair amount

<P>
The following details will prove useful to the Tutor:

<P>
<STRONG>Have you:</STRONG>
keyboard skills
<INPUT TYPE="checkbox" NAME="KEY" VALUE="key">

used a mouse
<INPUT TYPE="checkbox" NAME="MOUSE"
VALUE="mouse"> <BR>

used Windows 3.1
<INPUT TYPE="checkbox" NAME="WIN31"
VALUE="Win31">

used a word processor
<INPUT TYPE="checkbox" NAME="WP" VALUE="wp">

<P>
<H3>Have you any specific requirements?</H3>
<BR>

<TEXTAREA NAME="comments" ROWS=6
COLS=35>Enter specific requirements here.
</TEXTAREA>
<BR>

<INPUT TYPE="submit" VALUE="Submit Details">
<INPUT TYPE="reset">

</FORM>
</BODY>
```

Note the use of the <BR> and <P> tags to separate
one line of entries from the next. Also the user would
have to delete the text in the text area box before
typing in his/her own comment. Because the radio
button 'None' has CHECKED as an attribute, it will be
the one checked when displayed. It is not essential. If
the user selects another button, the one initially
displayed returns to the unchecked state. Finally, note
that the VALUE of the submit button ("Submit Details")
is printed on the submit button whereas the reset
button has the default wording "Reset".

Using Menus

In the following example, we demonstrate the use of
Menus using the <SELECT> tag. This has both a
starting and ending tag and takes the attribute NAME.

```
<SELECT NAME="course">
        <OPTION SELECTED> Word 6 Level 1
        <OPTION > Word 6 Level 2
        <OPTION > Ami Pro Level 1
        <OPTION > Ami Pro Level 2
</SELECT>
```

Figure 8.3 shows an example of a Menu.

```
<HEAD>
<TITLE>Registration for Courses</TITLE>
</HEAD>

<BODY>
<H3>To Register for One of the Following Courses</H3>
<P>
<STRONG>Please enter details and then select a course
from the list.</STRONG>

<P>
```

HTTP://TAKAGISM FASO-CS.COM/

YELLOW_CHAMBER.HTML

1581.33

```
<FORM METHOD=POST
ACTION="mailto:j.shelley@ic.ac.uk">

Please enter your name:
<INPUT TYPE="text" NAME="attendee" SIZE=40>

<P>
and your e-mail address:
<INPUT TYPE="text" NAME="mailadd" SIZE=30>

<P>
<SELECT NAME="course">
        <OPTION SELECTED> Word 6 Level 1
        <OPTION > Word 6 Level 2
        <OPTION > Ami Pro Level 1
        <OPTION > Ami Pro Level 2
</SELECT>

<INPUT TYPE="submit" VALUE="Submit Details">
<INPUT TYPE="reset">

</FORM>
</BODY>
```

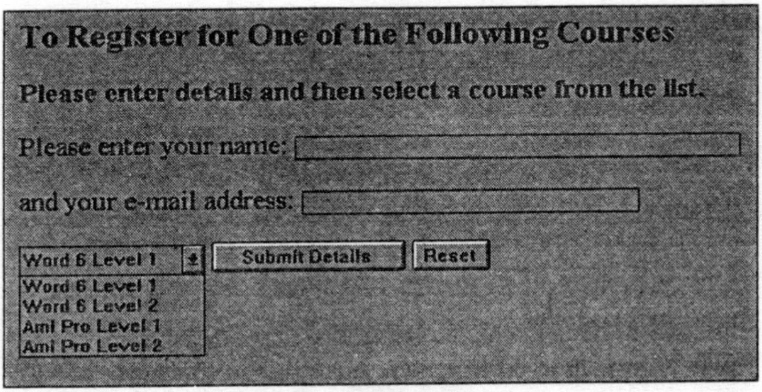

Figure 8.3

When the drop down list arrow is clicked, the list of courses is displayed. Note how the first option is selected in the drop down list because of the attribute SELECTED. Pre-selecting an option is optional. Note how the <SELECT> tag's NAME value ("course" above) will apply to any one of the options selected by the user. Like radio buttons they are mutually exclusive.

However, there is a MULTIPLE attribute which if present allows the user to select multiple values (see Figure 8.4 and how it appears in an e-mail message on page 82). When making multiple selections, it is often necessary to hold the Control key down as selections are clicked.

If the SIZE attribute is present with a value, see below, then this specifies the number of items to display, together with a scroll bar. But note well, if the MULTIPLE attribute is present, browsers choose a minimum SIZE greater than 1. They will not implement *your* SIZE value if it is less than this minimum.

<SELECT NAME="course" MULTIPLE SIZE=3>

How the Data is Sent

When the user clicks the submit button, the details are forwarded to the e-mail address specified in the FORM's ACTION attribute. These details take the general format of:

```
NAME=value
```

Each Name is separated by an ampersand symbol (&). For example, suppose the user had entered the data as shown in Figure 8.5:

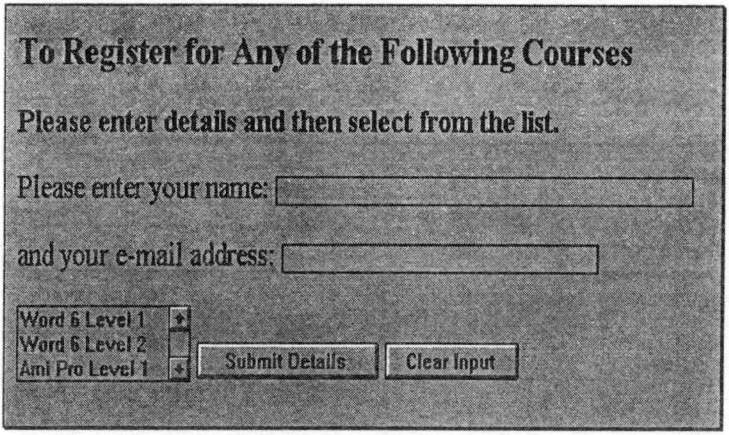

To Register for Any of the Following Courses

Please enter details and then select from the list.

Please enter your name: [   ]

and your e-mail address: [   ]

Word 6 Level 1	
Word 6 Level 2	
Ami Pro Level 1		**Submit Details**	**Clear Input**

Figure 8.4

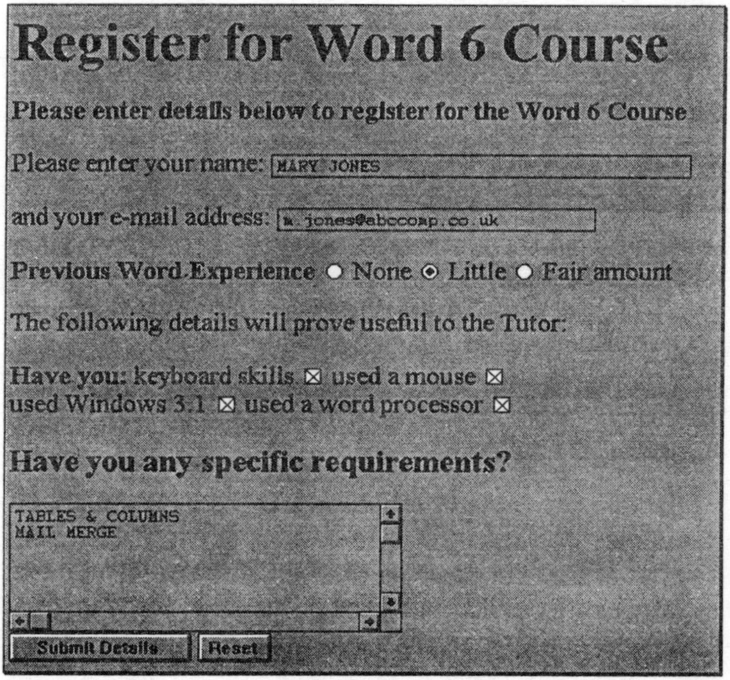

Register for Word 6 Course

Please enter details below to register for the Word 6 Course:

Please enter your name: [MARY JONES]

and your e-mail address: [m.jones@abccorp.co.uk]

Previous Word Experience ○ None ⊙ Little ○ Fair amount

The following details will prove useful to the Tutor:

Have you: keyboard skills ⊠ used a mouse ⊠
used Windows 3.1 ⊠ used a word processor ⊠

Have you any specific requirements?

```
TABLES & COLUMNS
MAIL MERGE
```

| **Submit Details** | **Reset** |

Figure 8.5

This is how it would appear in the e-mail message. Each NAME=value pair is separated by &. Spaces are replaced with the + symbol.

```
attendee=MARY+JONES&mailadd=m.jones@abcc
omp.co.uk&experience=Little&KEY=key&MOUS
E=mouse&WIN31=Win31&WP=wp&comments=TABLE
S+%26+COLUMNS%0D%0AMAIL+MERGE+%0D%0A
```

If no comment had been included *and* Mary Jones had taken the trouble to delete what was in the TEXTAREA box, then nothing would follow the equals sign after the Name value "comments=". Note also how the + symbol is used for spaces between Mary and Jones and the various spaces used in the textarea comment. Finally, note that the NAME is replaced by the variable name which the document author typed in as its value, so that:

```
<INPUT TYPE="text" NAME="attendee" SIZE=40>
```

becomes: `attendee=Mary+Jones`

The same applies to the VALUE attribute in radio buttons and checkboxes, where the NAME and VALUE are replaced by the author's variable names.

```
<INPUT TYPE="checkbox" NAME="KEY" VALUE="key">
```

becomes: `KEY=key`

The variable names do not have to be the same, but it is sometimes convenient to do this, in which case use upper and lower case to distinguish them. Since it is these names which are sent off as data, we may now appreciate why individual programs have to be written for each form. Here, of course, we have bypassed the need for a script or program.

The message string is difficult to read and the person receiving the message would need to manually adjust this string of data. I tend to copy and paste it into a word processor and then use a REPLACE feature to find '+' and replace it with a *nonbreaking space* character. Likewise, I use REPLACE to find all '&'s and replace them with the *manual line break*. I also recorded a macro to automate this task, calling it CTRL+S. Having selected the data string, I run the macro and the entire process is automated. Here is the result.

```
attendee=MARY JONES
mailadd=m.jones@abccomp.co.uk
experience=Little
KEY=key
MOUSE=mouse
WIN31=Win31
WP=wp
comments=TABLES %26 COLUMNS%0D%0AMAIL MERG
E %0D%0A
```

One e-mail program, stored the data string in the actual message. Another sent the data-string as an *attachment*. I had to call up the attachment directory in order to see the actual data. So there will be variations between browsers and e-mail programs as to where the data is stored. Matters will become more consistent in time.

What are the strange %26, etc.? These are ASCII characters typed in by the user but which cannot be printed by an e-mail program. It gives their equivalent hexadecimal number rather than the actual character. In the case of Mary Jones, she used the & (%26) and the *Enter key* (%0D) and a *line feed* (%0A) when typing in her comments. So yes, there will be a few strange characters to delete or perhaps replace in your word processor which is capable of displaying the ampersand (&).

Hexadecimal & Decimal

Appendix A lists the ASCII character set where the character number is given in decimal, the more usual approach. Many e-mail programs give the hexadecimal (base 16) equivalent. The % symbol is not part of the number, it is an e-mail sign denoting ASCII characters which it cannot display. Appendix B explains how to convert between hexadecimal and decimal, and vice versa, so that when necessary you can look up the ASCII character number and see what character it is meant to represent. (See also page 127.)

Data from MULTIPLE options in SELECT

In Figure 8.4, the user was invited to select one or more courses. This was achieved through the use of the MULTIPLE attribute in the SELECT tag. Suppose, the user had chosen Word 6 Levels 1 and 2 and Ami Pro Level 2, this is how it would appear in the e-mail message:

```
&course=Word+6+Level+1&course=Word+6+Level
+2&course=Ami+Pro+Level+2
```

Chapter 9

Tables & Columns - HTML 3

On the very first HTML course I was assisting at, one of the participants wanted to know how to create tables. It was most important for the material he was attempting to put on the Web. When told it was not going to be covered, since it is a version 3 HTML tag and consequently would not be supported by many browsers, he was most disappointed. However, we shall cover it here since this HTML element is currently being implemented by web browser developers, especially, Netscape, Arena, e-macs-w3 and some Mosaic versions. Future specifications should be backward compatible with what is mentioned in this chapter.

Be aware that some browsers will not be capable of displaying tables and may present the cell data as a string of words and phrases. For this reason, should you decide on using tables, it is advisable to have *two* versions. One for browsers which can display them, another for those that cannot. For the latter, you could resort to the use of the <PRE> tag using hyphens and the bar (|) symbol to create 'borders', and spaces to create 'columns' of cells.

On pages 89-90, an example of how to achieve this is given - both the source code and a Web page.

<TABLE>

Figure 9.1 shows a simple table. How is it coded in HTML? The entire table is enclosed in the non-empty pair - <TABLE> ... </TABLE> which can contain only

two tags: <CAPTION> and <TR> (table row). If a
<BORDER> attribute is included in the TABLE tag,
lines will be drawn around the cells.

<TR>

This non-empty tag defines one row in the table and
contains two elements - <TH> (table heading) and/or
<TD> (table data). The first table row tag specifies how
many cells in the row. All subsequent rows *must* have
the same number of cells as the first. Each row must
be terminated by the ending tag </TR> except for the
last where it is implied by the ending </TABLE> tag. It
is always better to include it.

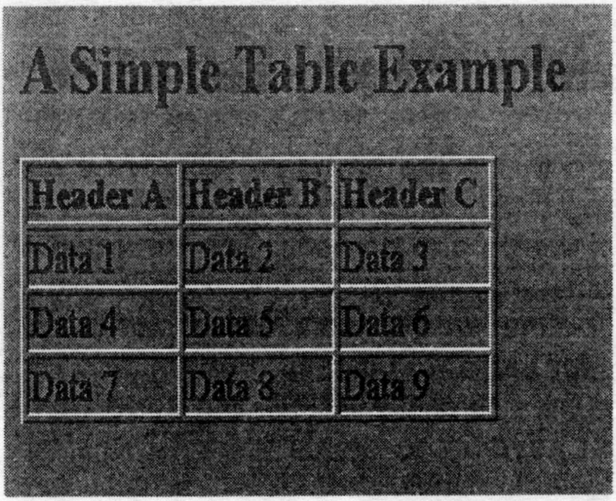

Figure 9.1

<TH> .. </TH> & <TD> .. </TD>

<TH> is used for the cell headings. It is identical in
syntax to <TD> which is used to specify what *data*
appears in each cell. The only difference is that most
browsers usually render the heading text differently to
<TD> text, typically in bold. Yes, building a table is a

chore. Each row and each cell and its data has to be typed as can be seen in the corresponding code for this example.

The <TH> tag is non-empty but the ending tag is optional since the end tag is implied by the next <TR>, <TH> or <TD> tag. Likewise, of course, for the <TD> tag. If either pair of tags contain no text then the corresponding cell is blank.

```
<HEAD>
<TITLE>  Simple Table Example</TITLE>
</HEAD>

<BODY>
<H2>A Simple Table Example</H2>

<TABLE BORDER>

<TR> <th> Header A </th> <th> Header B </th>
<th> Header C </th> </TR>

<TR> <td> Data 1 </td> <td> Data 2 </td>
<td> Data 3</td> </TR>

<TR> <td> Data 4 </td> <td> Data 5 </td>
<td> Data 6 </td> </TR>

<TR> <td> Data 7 </td> <td> Data 8 </td>
<td> Data 9 </td> </TR>

</TABLE>

</BODY>
```

<CAPTION>

Each table can have an optional CAPTION, which is centred across the table. It can contain text and images as well as hypertext.

85

```
<TABLE BORDER>
<CAPTION>Some Caption for a Table</CAPTION>
<TR> ... etc.
```

Some Effects Using Tables

By using the ROWSPAN and COLSPAN attributes within either <TH> or <TD>, you can specify how many cells can span a row or a column. For example, Figure 9.2. was achieved using the code below:

```
<BODY>
<H2>Spanning cells in a Table </H2>
<TABLE BORDER>
<CAPTION>Note How Cells span Rows and
Columns</CAPTION>

<TR> <th rowspan=2>LOGO <th colspan=2> Sales
</TR>
<TR> <td> 1995 <td> 1996 </TR>
<TR> <td> Data 1<td> Data 2 <td> Data 3 </TR>
<TR> <td> Data 4 <td>  </td> <td> Data 6 </TR>
<TR> <td colspan=3> Data 7 </TR>
<TR> <td> Data 8 <td colspan=2>Data 9 </TR>

</TABLE>

</BODY>
```

The LOGO spans 2 rows, taking up 1 column. "Sales" spans 2 columns. The first table row, therefore, specifies 3 columns in total. All other rows in the table must adhere to this number of cells.

"1995 and 1996" each occupy one column. They must go in columns 2 and 3 respectively of row 2, because LOGO already occupies the first column of row 2. Row 3 is normal but row 4 contains a blank cell in column 2.

Data 7 spans 3 columns in row 5, whilst Data 9 spans the last two columns of row 6.

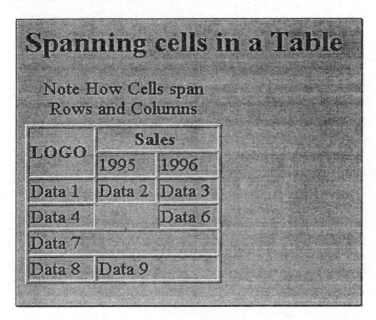

Figure 9.2

Replacing the text *LOGO* with an <IMG> element would have placed the image in the first two rows of column 1. Inserted between <A> tags would have made it a hypertext image.

```
<TR> <th rowspan=2><A HREF="somedoc.html">
<IMG SRC="company_logo.gif"></A>
 <th colspan=2> Sales </TR>
```

87

Text in Columns Using Tables

Tables may be used to create columns of text as shown in Figure 9.3.

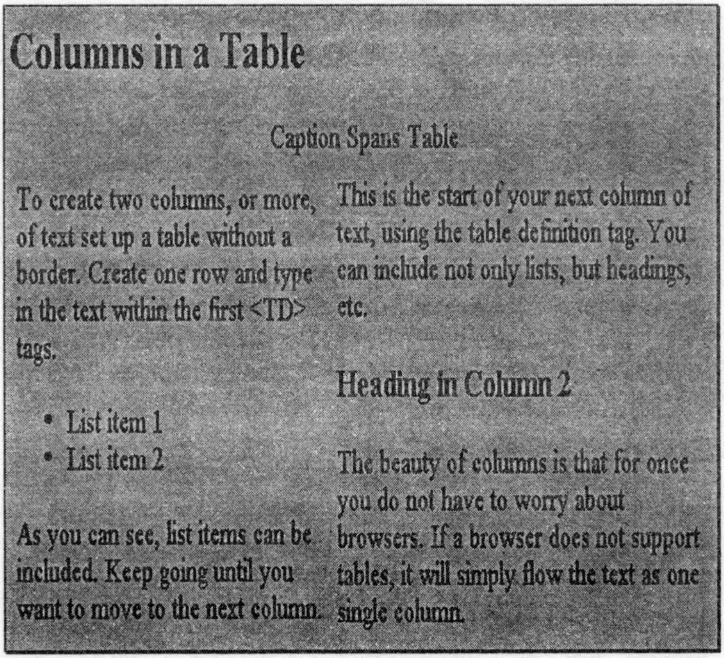

Columns in a Table

Caption Spans Table

To create two columns, or more, of text set up a table without a border. Create one row and type in the text within the first <TD> tags.

- List item 1
- List item 2

As you can see, list items can be included. Keep going until you want to move to the next column.

This is the start of your next column of text, using the table definition tag. You can include not only lists, but headings, etc.

Heading in Column 2

The beauty of columns is that for once you do not have to worry about browsers. If a browser does not support tables, it will simply flow the text as one single column.

Figure 9.3

```
<HEAD>
<TITLE>  Column Example</TITLE>
</HEAD>

<BODY>
<H2>Columns in a Table </H2>
<TABLE>
<CAPTION>Caption Spans Table</CAPTION>
<TR>
```

88

```
<td> To create two columns, or more, of text set up a
table without a border. Create one row and type in the
text within the first &lt;TD&gt; tags.
<UL>
        <LI>List item 1
        <LI>List item 2
</UL
<P> As you can see, list items can be included.
Keep going until you want to move to the next column.
</td>
<td>
This is the start of your next column of text, using the
table definition tag.You can include not only lists, but
headings, etc.

<H3>Heading in Column 2</H3>

The beauty of columns is that for once you do not
have to worry about browsers. If a browser does not
support tables, it will simply flow the text as one single
column. </td>

</TR>
</TABLE>

</BODY>
```

For Browsers which do not support Tables

Here is one method for testing a user's browser.

```
<H3>Performance Table for 1995/96.</H3>
```

If you can see a table after this paragraph, then your
browser supports Tables. If you do not see the table,
then click

```
<A HREF="text_alternative.html"> text version </A>
```
to obtain the text version equivalent of this document.

```
<CENTER><TABLE BORDER>
<TR> <th colspan=2>Performance 1995/96 </th>
</TR>

<TR>
<TH> 1995 </th> <th> 1996 </th>
</TR>

<TR> <td> 1234</td> <td> 2345 </td>
</TR>

<TR> <td> 3456 </td> <td> 4567 </td>
</TR>

</TABLE> </CENTER>¹
</BODY>
```

Performance Table for 1995/96.

If you can see a table after this paragraph, then your
browser supports Tables. If you do not see the table, then
click text version to obtain the text version equivalent of
this document.

Performance 1995/96	
1995	1996
1234	2345
3456	4567

---

[1] The non-empty <CENTER> tag can be used to centre anything it
contains. See page 125. Note American spelling of the tag name.

Chapter 10

Design & Style

> ### *Some Design Considerations*

HTML is quite easy to use and there is a danger that we rush into constructing our pages without due consideration to the end result. The overriding consideration is that there are many different Web browsers in use from full blown graphical, sound and video browsers to very simple line browsers. What you see on *your* Web page may look very different on another browser. If we remember this all the time, then we can design pages which will look reasonable on any browser.

Keep it Simple

This is one of the first laws of programming and applies equally to HTML. Provided you keep to the tags discussed in this book, then most browsers will have no problem in displaying pages along the lines *you* intend. Version 3 features cannot be interpreted by all browsers and are better avoided for the time being.

Using the tags mentioned in this text will ensure attractive enough documents so that you can put your effort into the *content* rather than the format of a page. After all, the reason people will want to read your pages is to get information not pages full of images and pictures. For that they can turn to magazines.

Under Construction

Very few of us are ever 100% happy with the layout and content of our Web pages. We can spend a great deal of time 'improving' sentences, layout, etc. But it is better to put something out rather than delay matters and put out nothing at all. For this reason, it is very common to see phrases such as "Under Construction" or "Work in Progress" on Web pages. This informs the readers that it is not quite complete - you should not be embarrassed to do the same.

Signatures

All home pages and other major pages should have your full name, your e-mail address and a date, commonly referred to as a *signature*. This adds authority to your work. It also provides a means whereby readers can send comments about your pages. The benefits gained in this way frequently far outweigh any negative responses from readers.

When a date is added, make sure that you do not use all numbers since some countries use a MM/DD/YY format whilst others use the DD/MM/YY format. 5/6/96, therefore, becomes ambiguous. Use 5/June/96 or something similar. I was interested to see that this latter convention has been adopted by certain sites over the last year where previously they had used only digits in their earlier works.

Dates are useful so that readers can see how up-to-date the material is. Any later refinements you make can include updating the date stamp. However, even if you do not make any changes, you ought to keep changing the date stamp on a regular basis. There is nothing worse than readers seeing something dated in

1994. It leaves them wondering how valid the material is. Has the author dropped dead or moved from the organisation and no one has thought to delete or take over the document?

Signatures are usually placed at the end of the page together with a message stating whether the material is 'protected' by copyright or not.

Theft

Do not be afraid to 'borrow' other design styles which you come across and admire. Most browsers allow readers to view the HTML source of the page they are looking at. This is also a good way to learn how to use the HTML language. You can copy and paste the source into an editor and edit the existing material by replacing the original with your own information. Of course, it is not allowed to use the original material in your own pages. But the style, design, layout or whatever, can be borrowed. However, if you do this make certain that the author has not used any HTML 3 features or, indeed, any older and obsolete tags.

Avoid using *any* material where there is a strict copyright message attached, or from organisations with large funds and a virulent legal department. If you do borrow style, you should have the grace to acknowledge the fact on your own pages.

For Windows users, you may find this tip useful. When viewing source code in Netscape, clicking on Edit and Copy tends to de-select the View Source window, making it impossible to do a copy and paste. However, if when viewing the source you select the text and press CTRL+C, this does allow the selected text to be copied to the Windows clipboard for subsequent pasting.

Images

Loading images can be time consuming, much longer than loading text since the files themselves tend to be larger than text files. Once the document *text* has been loaded, the browser then has to request copies of the image files and load them into the document. The TCP/IP protocol[1] tends to transfer data in small units called *packets*. The larger the file the more packets have to be transferred.[2]

With the increasing traffic on the Internet, the channel bandwidths which are carrying these packets are in danger of becoming congested. It is becoming a common practice for pages to carry a small image which can be clicked on to reveal a larger version should the reader so desire. This has the advantage of faster loading times and reducing the traffic over the Internet. Here is an example, where a small image is downloaded onto the page with a URL reference to a larger version:

```
Click <A HREF="Large_cat.gif">
<IMG SRC="small_cat.gif" ALT="My Cat"
ALIGN=middle></A>
to see a larger copy of my cat (90K bytes).
```

Should someone want to see a larger version of "My Cat", they are invited to click the image. Those who are

---

[1] See Glossary.
[2] More details in "The Internet and the World Wide Web explained", by J. Shelley, published by Bernard Babani, book No. BP403.

not will not be infuriated by waiting for the large version to be displayed on their screens. It is also good etiquette to inform the reader of the size of file that has to be downloaded - 90K bytes in the above example.

Note also the use of the ALT="My Cat" which will be seen by those users without a graphics browser. Without the ALT attribute, many would simply see the default text [IMAGE] - not very helpful. Whilst talking about users with non-graphical browsers, it is becoming customary to provide two versions of a document, a graphical and a text version. See under FORMs below for more details.

Using <TITLE>

Automatic programs called *web crawlers, spiders, robots* - amongst other terms - trawl the Web looking at Titles, Headings, URLs and compile databases from them.[3] Should you want your document to be included in these databases, add a <TITLE> tag within the <HEAD> of your document. Suppose it contained the word *dinosaurs*. Someone searching for documents on dinosaurs would be able to see your document in the list provided by a robot which compiles databases from keywords in <TITLE>s.

FORMs

Not all browsers can cope with forms so you may wish to provide an alternative text version. Since all browsers are supposed to ignore tags which they

---

[3] Try: http://web.nexor.co.uk/mak/doc/robots/robots.html for more information.

cannot recognise, your document may look odd. In the following code, you can see how to overcome this.

```
<H3>Please fill in the following form.</H3>

<FORM ACTION="No_action">
If you can see a button enclosed in square brackets at
the end of this sentence, then your browser supports
Forms.

--[<INPUT TYPE="checkbox" NAME="chkbutton"
VALUE="on" CHECKED>]--

If you do not see the button, then click
<A HREF="text_alternative.html"> text version </A>
to obtain the text version equivalent of this document.
</FORM>
```

Please fill in the following form.

If you can see a button enclosed in square
brackets at the end of this sentence, then your
browser supports Forms. --[⊠]-- If you do
not see the button, then click text version to
obtain the text version equivalent of this
document.

Note that because there is no <INPUT TYPE = "submit"> this Form will not send off any input data. It is simply there to test the capability of the browser. If users see a checkbox then all well and good, if not they select the text version.

Design of Home Pages

A good home page will welcome readers, let them know where they are and what interesting information they have access to. It is the starting point for the reader and should contain such details as:

- your name & site
- who maintains the document
- what the document is about
- a list of contents which can be explored
- signature: name, e-mail and date stamp

Some Design Considerations

The following are suggestions, at least enough to make you consider various points.

Keep it Short & Concise

The Home page should be small so that the reader can have it loaded quickly and then decide where to go from there. It should not contain large images which will take time to load and make the reader despair. I have frequently given up waiting for home pages to be displayed, and decide to return some other day when I can afford the time to wait, which probably means that I never do. If you must include graphics, then make them small.

The information should be informative but not long winded ramblings. The detailed information can come from your other pages. Clearly, the home page must have links to other documents which ideally ought to be kept in the same folder/directory as the home page so that relative links can be established.

Link Back to the Home Page

Once a reader has been allowed to load another page, it makes sense to have a link back to the home page. If one page leads on to another, then include links back to the previous and/or to the home page.

This is especially important if the reader visits a page directly, having found its URL from somewhere, without going through your home page. Links back to the home page under these circumstances will give the reader the opportunity of visiting the home page directly.

Likewise, if you have a long document with many *sections* which have separate links to various parts of the document, a "Return to Top of Page" hyperlink enables the reader to get back to the top of the document quickly. Typically, the top may be a list of Contents.

Multiple Links

If your home page or any other major page has many hyperlinks, you may need to give some thought as to how they should appear. It is often confusing to readers when links are scattered within paragraphs of text. It may be better to keep them together in a list using <UL> as shown below. Which of the following would you prefer to read?

Here are some references which you may like to look at: An Introduction to HTML is a good starting point. Whereas Further Features examines some of the HTML version 3 tags. Another useful document is The Design and Style of HTML documents. Yet more information can be found in Advanced Use of Forms.

Here are some references which you may like to look at:
- An Introduction to HTML is a good starting point.
- Further Features examines some of the HTML version 3 tags.
- Another useful document is The Design and Style of HTML documents.
- Yet more information can be found in Advanced Use of Forms.

```
<BODY>
Here are some references which you may like to look
at:
<P>
<UL>

   <LI> <A HREF="intro.html">
 An Introduction to HTML </A> is a good starting point.

   <LI> <A HREF="fur_feats.html">Further Features
</A>
examines some of the HTML version 3 tags.

   <LI>Another useful document is
<A HREF= "design.html">The Design and Style of
HTML documents.</A>

   <LI>Yet more information can be found in
<A HREF="adv.html"> Advanced Use of Forms.</A>
</UL>
```

Do Not Let your Visitors Escape

One frequent oddity about some home pages is that they list sites and documents other than their own. This will allow the reader to click on these and be whisked off to some other site without having had the time or opportunity to explore your own information. They may never return!

Organising Your Documents

If you are involved in several different projects, or whatever, it makes sense to organise the files into separate directories or folders.

Let us say that we are working on three separate projects (or goods that our company is promoting, or information about departments in a university). One useful practice is to have a separate folder for each of the three projects. Project 1 in one folder with its documents and associated image files, Project 2 in another, etc.

Moving one set of project files from one location to another is now a much simpler task. We are less likely to overlook one or two of the associated files referred to by relative address links.

Chapter 11

Creating Web Documents

There are many ways of creating HTML documents and of viewing the result on a Web browser. One method commonly used is to type the HTML code into your own word processor, such as Word 6, Ami-Pro or WordPerfect 6.1. However, this file needs to be saved as an ASCII or text only file. For example on Word 6, choose:

- File, Save As
- click the drop down arrow on Save File As Type
- select Text Only
- type in a name with an .htm extension and click OK
- then Close the document

Some, if not all, browsers are not able to open a file which is already open in some other application. When you close the file, you may initially be told that the "document contains formatting which cannot be saved in text format. Do you want to save changes?" Choose the No option.

You can then call up your web browser and open that file. In Netscape, this is the File, Open File option. You locate the directory where the file is stored and open it. You will then see the document as others using the same browser will see it.

The .htm extension is required by Windows 3.1 users due to the limitation of the MSDOS three-letter file extension. However, your Web master will be in a position to change this to the more usual `.html` extension when the document is finally loaded onto the network Web server. Most servers are more amenable to the number of characters in a file name.

Whilst viewing the Web page, errors, if any, will become obvious as well as any poor design features. A quick way to check your source before returning to your word processor is to use the *View Source* option if supported by your browser. This enables you to view the source code and the incorrect Web display at the same time. Having noted the errors, go back to the original HTML document using your word processor, make your changes, save it as text only again, and view the document again.

Once satisfied with the display, it has now to be stored on the network server's file storage system. It is common in many LANs for this to be done by one person, usually known as the *Web Master*. He or she will be responsible for vetting and maintaining what goes on the Web server.

The web master will supply you with a URL so that you can tell the world how to locate your document. It will contain the *http* protocol, the Web *site* address, the *directory* it is stored in and the *name* of your document. In this way, and with permission from the web master, you can create your own home pages.

Create a Template

It is also useful to create a basic template as follows:

```
<HTML>
<HEAD>
```

102

```
<TITLE> --- </TITLE>
<BASE HREF="...">
</HEAD>

<BODY>
<IMG SRC="comp_logo.gif" ALT="Company Logo">
<ADDRESS>
Last updated by Joe Public on July, 1996 (e-mail:
j.public@abc.co.uk)
</ADDRESS>
</BODY>
</HTML>
```

Company logos could also be included. This 'template'
should be saved as text only. When you next open this
file, open it as Read Only so that you cannot
inadvertently overwrite it.

Common Errors

Here are some of the common errors made even by
experienced HTML practitioners.

Failure to include both double quotes where required.
This is particularly common for HREF URLs. Some
browsers will 'correct' the error, others cannot.

Failure to include the closing > for a tag or to add a
space before the closing angle bracket. Since
browsers tend to ignore things they do not understand,
the text which follows may be formatted according to
whatever tag was previously in effect.

Failure to add the closing slash (/) in an end tag or
putting spaces around the slash will cause problems.

Missing out the semi-colon in a character entity (< for <) will cause problems, too.

Perhaps one of the most common errors is the misuse of the <P> tag. It should not be used with those tags which imply their own paragraph tags, for example with headings, ADDRESS, BLOCKQUOTE or PRE.

<P> tags should not be used with list item tags <LI>, <DT> or <DD> since these also imply their own paragraph breaks. But there is one instance where it is legal, that is with the last of the above. Yes, this does seem confusing so let us clarify the situation.

It is illegal to have more than one <DD> following a definition term <DT>. This implies that you can have but one definition description <DD>. If this requires more than one paragraph, however, the correct way is to insert the <P> tag. In that way, your one definition description may contain multiple paragraphs.

Chapter 12

Frames in HTML

Frames divide a Web screen into multiple windows, with each window presenting a different page of information. Indeed, we have already been using "frames" so far except that our Web pages have consisted of only one frame.

To create a Web page comprising more than one frame, a separate document is required which consists of two tags:

- a FRAMESET tag which specifies how many frames to create
- FRAME tags, one for each frame, to specify the content of each frame

Thus, if you wish to create a Web page consisting of two frames, *three* files would be required. A frame file (specifying the number of frames via the FRAMESET tag plus FRAME tags containing the URLs to their contents) and two more normal HTML documents one for each frame. In this text, the former will be referred to as a *frame document*.

Syntax for the Frame document

A frame document consists of a non-empty FRAMESET tag which specifies the *number* and *size* of each frame and empty FRAME tags which specify the address of ordinary HTML files which each frame will contain. A frame document has no BODY tag.

```
<HTML>
<HEAD>     </HEAD>

<FRAMESET ROWS= "50%,50%">
.....<FRAME SRC="url">
.....<FRAME SRC="url">
</ FRAMESET>
</HTML>
```

a basic frame document specifying two horizontal frames, each occupying 50% of the window height

FRAMESET tag

It takes one of the following attributes: ROWS or COLS. The number of *values* after the attribute specify the **number** of rows (or columns) and each *value* specifies the **size** of each row (or column). Thus, the following code would create three separate *horizontal* frames (rows)

Frame A - 25% high
Frame B - 50% high
Frame C - 25% high

<FRAMESET ROWS= "25%, 50%, 25%">

The first will take up 25% of the total window, the second 50% and the last 25%. Note how the combined total percentage adds up to 100% and that each value is separated by a comma and enclosed in double quotes. The following code would create three vertical frames (columns).

<FRAMESET COLS = "20%, 50%,30%">

Frame A 20% wide	Frame B 50% wide	Frame C 30% wide

The ROWS Attribute

The ROWS attribute specifies a horizontal frame and the *value* specifies its *height* not its width since that is determined by the size of the browser window set by the user.

ROWS takes one or more of three types of *values*:

- a simple number referring to a number of pixels[1] - e.g. 100
- a percentage of the *remaining* space - a number with the % symbol, e.g. 35%
- an asterisk which takes up all the space left over after the other two types have been evaluated

Thus: <FRAMESET ROWS = "100, *, 35%"> would establish a horizontal frame of 100 pixels high, another which takes up

---

[1] Pixel is short for "picture element", i.e. all the little screen squares which make up a complete picture. 96 pixels is *about* 1 inch square on a 1024×768 resolution screen.

35% of the *remaining* space and a middle frame which would fill up whatever space is left over.

Pixel Values

If a pixel value is used, the row height will always be fixed at that height. This is the least controllable type of value to use unless other types are also included. Pixels values are always specified by a simple number.

Percentage Values

These are numbers followed by the % symbol and are limited to numbers from 1% to 100%. A row defined by a percentage value will have a *height* which fills *n%* of the window not used by other rows defined with pixel values. If all values in a row have percentages, each will take up *n%* of the window size and in a ratio-proportion of the window size.

Assuming a row contains only percentage values, should the total values not add up to 100%, each value is proportionally increased or decreased to make up 100%.

The Asterisk wildcard Value

This is sometimes called a *wildcard variable* and consists of an asterisk. The frame it refers to is assigned whatever space is left over after pixel and/or % values have been evaluated. However, should there not be enough room left over then the wildcard row may not appear (in some cases it may be reduced to 2 or 3 pixels). For example:

<FRAMESET ROWS = "100, 40%, * ,39%" > would not leave much room, if any, for the third wildcard row.

If there are multiple wildcard variables, then the remaining space is allocated evenly between them. When a number precedes the asterisk, for example, 2*, that frame gets more space. Thus: "2*, *" would give 2/3rds of the space to the first and 1/3rd to the second.

The COLS Attribute

Identical to the ROWS attribute except that vertical frames are being described and their *values* refer to the *width* of the frames, their heights being controlled by the window size.

It is not common to include both the ROWS and the COLS attributes in the same FRAMESET tag. It can be done but beware! and see the example on page 118.

The FRAME tag

FRAME tags are placed after the FRAMESET tag. There must be one for each frame defined in the FRAMESET tag. FRAME is an empty tag and can take the following attributes:

```
<FRAME   SRC="URL"
         NAME= "a"
         MARGINWIDTH= "p"
         MARGINHEIGHT= "p"
         SCROLLING= "yes" | "no" | "auto"
         NORESIZE>
```

A Simple Example:

```
<FRAMESET ROWS = "50%, 50%">
  <FRAME SRC = "frameA.htm">
  <FRAME SRC = "frameB.htm">
</FRAMESET>
```

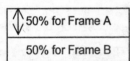

50% for Frame A

50% for Frame B

Since there are two frames described by the ROWS attribute, so there must be two HTML documents each one referenced by a FRAME tag.

SRC attribute

This attribute provides the location of the document to be placed in a particular frame. The source may be an HTML file, a JPEG or GIF file, etc. The syntax is the same as that of the HREF and SRC attributes for the <A> and <IMG> tags respectively.

If a FRAME tag has no SRC attribute, the frame it refers to is left blank but this can look ugly when displayed on the Web. It is always sensible to have a URL even if this is a reference to an empty file with just a background colour (see page 127).

We shall look at the other attributes after we have completed Exercise 1.

Exercise 1

We shall create three vertical frames. The <HTML> tags and frequently the <HEAD> tags will not always be included in some of the following code examples.

Frame document - *Ex1_Fset.htm* [2]

```
<HEAD>
<TITLE> "A Simple 3 Column" EX1_Fset.htm
</TITLE>
</HEAD>

<FRAMESET COLS= "33%,33%,33%">
      <FRAME SRC="Ex1_left.htm">
      <FRAME SRC= "Ex1_mid.htm">
      <FRAME SRC= "Ex1_right.htm">
</FRAMESET>
```

Left Frame   *Ex1_left.htm*

```
<HEAD>
<TITLE>Ex1_left.htm  for left frame </TITLE>
</HEAD>

<BODY>
<!-- This goes into Left Frame -->
<H1>Contents for Left</H1>
<H3>Left Frame of the simple 3-columns</H3>
<ADDRESS>John Shelley<BR>
Test Case<BR>
Ex1_left.htm</ADDRESS>
</BODY>
```

Middle Frame *Ex1_mid.htm*

```
<HEAD>
<TITLE>Ex1_mid.htm  for middle frame </TITLE>
</HEAD>

<BODY>
<!-- This goes into Middle Frame -->
<H1>Contents for Middle</H1>
<H3>Middle Frame of the simple 3-columns</H3>
```

---

[2] For the sake of clarity, I take advantage of Windows 95 long names for all file names. Those using Windows 3.1 will be limited to 8.3 character structure for names.

```
<ADDRESS>John Shelley<BR>
Test Case<BR>
Ex1_mid.htm</ADDRESS></BODY>
```

Right Frame *Ex1_right.htm*
```
<BODY>
<!-- This goes into Right Frame -->
<H1>Contents for Right</H1>
<H3>Right Frame of the simple 3-columns</H3>
<ADDRESS>John Shelley<BR>
Test Case<BR>
Ex1_right.htm</ADDRESS></BODY>
```

The MARGINWIDTH & MARGINHEIGHT attributes

These control the margins of your frame. Their values are simple numbers specifying a number of pixels between the border and the frame's content. MARGINWIDTH specifies the amount of space on the *left* margin, MARGINHEIGHT specifies the amount of space for the *top* margin. You control, therefore, only the left and top margins. (Other sources state that they control *both* top/bottom and left/right margins.)

```
<FRAMESET ROWS = "50%,50%">
  <FRAME SRC = "frameA.htm"  MARGINWIDTH= "30"
    MARGINHEIGHT= "15">
  <FRAME SRC = "frameB.htm"  MARGINWIDTH= "15"
    MARGINHEIGHT= "30">
</FRAMESET>
```

The above would result in two rows of equal size with the first frame's contents (A) pushed 30 pixels to the right and 15 pixels down; the second frame's content (B) would be pushed 15 pixels to the right and 30 down.

Notes:

1. If a frame's content extends below or to the right of the frame, scroll bars will automatically appear to allow readers to see the rest of the contents.

2. Margins settings cannot be less than 1 since contents are not allowed to touch a border [3]. If margins are set too deep so that none of the contents are visible, the browser will ignore your settings.

3. Both attributes are optional. The browser will determine appropriate settings when they are not used.

4. Background colour and patterns used in the HTML source document are not affected by the margin attributes and will fill the *entire* frame.

SCROLLING attribute

If the frame's content cannot be contained within the frame, scroll bars will appear automatically. However, you can set the SCROLLING attribute to one of three values: "yes", "no" or "auto".

SCROLLING = "yes" means that scroll bars will *always* appear whether they are needed or not.

SCROLLING = "no" means that they will not appear, regardless of whether the contents are fully visible or not.

SCROLLING = "auto" means show the scroll bars if needed, otherwise ignore. It is the default assumed by the browser if this attribute is not used.

NORESIZE attribute

Normally, a user can drag on a frame border to resize it. But if the NORESIZE attribute is present, it prevents the user from being able to resize the border. It takes no *value*.

Note: Navigator 3.0 places a small dot in the centre of frame border which can be resized. At present, lower versions of Netscape and Internet Explorer do not.

---

[3] But see page 124 for MS Internet Explorer!

111

Exercise 2

Here we shall use some of the files already created, but the middle one will contain an anchor link to another document. This other document will replace the existing one. It will also contain a link back to the original.

Middle Column calls up another HTML document to replace it

Frame document - *Ex2_Fset.htm*

```
<FRAMESET COLS= "33%,33%,33%">
  <FRAME SRC="Ex1_left.htm">
  <FRAME SRC= "Ex2_mid_ALINK.htm">     new document
  <FRAME SRC= "Ex1_right.htm">
</FRAMESET>
```

New Middle Frame Document - *Ex2_mid_ALINK.htm*

```
<BODY>
<!-- Goes into middle Frame and contains a
hyperlink to another file in an Anchor tag -->
<H1>Contents for New Middle</H1>
<H3>Middle Frame of the simple 3-columns</H3>
<A HREF="REPLACE_mid.htm">Click here to
    replace MIDDLE FRAME</A>
<ADDRESS>John Shelley<BR>
Test Case<BR>
Ex2_mid_ALINK.htm</ADDRESS></BODY>
```

This Replaces the Middle Frame and provides a link back to it *Replace_mid.htm*

```
<BODY>
<!-- This replaces the middle Frame with a fox
cub gif file. Called by Ex2_mid_ALINK.htm -->
<H3>Replaced Contents for Middle</H3>
<H3>Here is a Fox Cub</H3>
<IMG SRC="foxcub.gif">
<P>
<ADDRESS>John Shelley<BR>
Test Case<BR>
REPLACE_mid.htm</ADDRESS>
<A HREF="Ex2_mid_ALINK.htm">Return to
    original</A>
</BODY>
```

112

Target Practice

So far, we have seen how a hypertext link in a frame will replace its contents with another file. It is identical to a normal HTML document which replaces the full screen with another page. However, with frames, only one frame window is affected; the others are not affected.

When using a TARGET attribute, it is possible for the user to click a hypertext link in one frame and cause the HTML file to appear in another frame (the *target*) rather than replace the existing frame's content. This is useful when the existing frame is a list of contents which should remain visible all the time.

In the following, let us say that we have a list of contents in frame A. When an item is clicked, it will appear in the middle frame, leaving frames A and C unaltered. This is achieved via a combination of a *target* attribute in the hypertext link and a *name* attribute in its FRAME tag, thus:

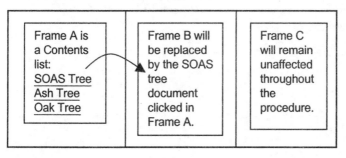

Frame A is a Contents list:
SOAS Tree
Ash Tree
Oak Tree

Frame B will be replaced by the SOAS tree document clicked in Frame A.

Frame C will remain unaffected throughout the procedure.

Exercise 3:
Frame Document   *Ex3_Fset.htm*

```
<FRAMESET COLS= "33%,33%,33%">
   <FRAME SRC="Ex3_Contents_Frame.htm">
   <FRAME SRC= "Ex3_Middle_Frame.htm"
     NAME="Ex3_middle">4
   <FRAME SRC= "Ex3_Right_Frame.htm">
</FRAMESET>
```

---

[4] On my platform, Office 97, all names used were *case sensitive* in both the Name tag and the Target tags. If I changed case, I was rewarded with a blank screen!

The *name* attribute allows the middle frame to become a target for another file.

Here are the three HTML files for frames A, B & C.

Left frame - *Contents* - Stays Put!
Ex3_Contents_Frame.htm

```
<BODY>
<!-- This goes into Left frame as the Contents
list. It has a link to target the middle
Frame.-->
<H1>Contents</H1>
<H3><A HREF="Ex3_Target_Middle.htm"
    TARGET="Ex3_middle">SOAS Tree </A></H3>
<H3>Ash Tree</H3>
<H3>Oak Tree</H3>
<ADDRESS>John Shelley<BR>
Test Case<BR>
Ex3_Contents_Frame.htm</ADDRESS></BODY>
```

Middle - original - but destined to be the TARGET for another file *Ex3_Middle_Frame.htm*

```
<BODY>
<!-- This goes into the Middle frame and has
an image of a girl with a pearl. It will be
replaced by another file when the SOAS tree
link is clicked in the Left frame.-->
<H3>Middle Frame becomes the Target</H3>
Here is Jan Vermeer's <I>Girl with a Pearl</I>
<P>
<IMG SRC="girlpearl_JV.jpg"></P>
<ADDRESS>John Shelley<BR>
Test Case<BR>
Ex3_Middle_Frame.htm</ADDRESS></BODY>
```

Right original & it will not change
Ex3_Right_frame.htm

```
<BODY>
<!-- This goes into the Right frame and has an
earth.gif image. It will be replaced by
another file from the left contents frame
when Soas tree is clicked..-->
<H3>Right Frame remains static</H3>
```

```
<H4>I shall stay here, looking good and not
change.</H4>
Here is the earth.gif.<P>
<IMG SRC="earth.gif"></P>
<ADDRESS>John Shelley<BR>
Test Case<BR>
Ex3_Right_Frame.htm</ADDRESS></BODY>
```

When the hypertext link in the left frame is clicked, the following
HTML file is placed it in the target frame "Ex3_Middle".

**The Target file for Middle - It will replace the above
middle frame *Ex3_Target_Middle.htm***
```
<BODY>
<!-- This file will be TARGETed for the
Middle frame when the SOAS tree link is
clicked in the Left frame.-->
<H3>I am destined for the Middle Frame</H3>
<H4>I am the Soas Tree</H4><P>
<IMG SRC="soas.gif"></P>
<Address>John Shelley<BR>
Test Case<BR>
B_Target_Middle.htm</Address>
<A HREF="Ex3_Middle_Frame.htm">Return to
Original middle Frame Contents</A>
</BODY>
```

Note that this frame has included a hypertext link which will
restore the original middle frame's content. This is like the
example in Exercise 2, where a link in a frame replaces its
contents.

It may take a little thought to appreciate how all this works. One
way, which might help, is to work out a layout structure, give
each frame file a sensible name and then create the frame
document. For example:

- Frame Left original (with a *Target* tag in the Anchor tag)
- Frame Middle original
- Frame Right original
- Frame Middle - the new one aimed at the original frame
  Middle
- create the Frameset (with a *Name* tag to the target)

NAME attribute

This attribute is placed in the FRAME tag of the frame document. Its purpose is to provide a name for a frame which is destined to become the target of another HTML file. Note that target names **must** begin with an alphabetic character and **must not** begin with the underscore character since the latter is used for reserved *target* names. See page 121.

Other places to put the TARGET attribute

The TARGET attribute may be placed in:

> an <A> tag, as described above
> a <BASE> tag
> a <FORM> tag
> an <AREA> tag[5]

In the BASE tag

When this tag is used, ***all*** links will be targeted to the named frame. But before I tell you, in which file do you think the BASE tag with the TARGET attribute has to go?

<BASE TARGET="frame_name">

It is customary for the BASE tag to appear immediately after the BODY tag and it must go *in the HTML document which has the links to the targeted frame*. Thus, if frame A were a contents' list and must remain unchanged, yet has links targeted to a frame B, the BASE tag would have to be placed in the Frame A document. *All* links in Frame A would now be targeted to frame B. This saves having to include a TARGET attribute in each <A> tag.

```
<BASE TARGET="B_frame">
  <A HREF="link1.htm"></A>
  <A HREF="link2.htm"></A>
  <A HREF="link3.htm"></A>
  <A HREF="link4.htm"  TARGET="C_frame"></A>
```
all these would be targeted into the *B_frame*

but the fourth file is aimed at the *C-frame*!

---

[5] Not covered in this text but it behaves in a similar fashion to the anchor tag. It is used for mapping an image with different urls for each part of the image.

It is possible to override the BASE target using the target attribute in an anchor tag. Thus, in the above code, a contents list in frame A with four links could target frame B for three of them, but if the fourth link had an anchor target to frame C, then that link would be placed in frame C. Of course, both frames would have to be NAMEd in the frame document.

In the FORM tag

It behaves in a similar fashion to the TARGET attribute in an anchor tag.

```
<FORM ACTION="url" METHOD=POST TARGET="left-frame">
```

Any results sent back by the CGI script will now be targeted into the *left_frame*. Such use of the TARGET tag in the FORM tag could be useful to allow users to correct errors without having to go back and forth between Web pages. One frame will contain their entry form; the targeted frame will display any results sent back; and both can be viewed simultaneously.

NOFRAMES tag

This tag is useful for specifying what to do for those browsers which do not have 'frames capability'. It is a non-empty tag which can incorporate any HTML tag including the <BODY> tag, indeed, it should contain a *body* tag.

The NOFRAMES tag may be placed immediately after the first <FRAMESET> tag or after the last </FRAMESET> tag. The latter makes code more readable. Frames capable browsers are geared to completely ignore the NOFRAMES tags and all they contain.

```
<HEAD>
<TITLE> ABC </TITLE></HEAD>

<FRAMESET>etc.....
</FRAMESET>

<NOFRAMES>
        <BODY>
                etc...what to do if frames are not supported....
        </BODY>
</NOFRAMES>
```

Using both the ROWS & COLS attributes

Look at the following:

`<FRAMESET ROWS = "50%, 25%,25%" COLS = "50%,50%" >`

Here we have included both attributes, 3 rows and 2 columns. This would result[6] in 3x2 frames, requiring six separate HTML files *plus* the frameset document.

50% Col=50%	Col=50%
25%	
25%	

When both attributes are used, the result is a grid of y rows × z cols. Each section becomes a separate frame each requiring its own FRAME tag. The use of both attributes in the hands of a graphic artist can result in some fine artistic work. One site is as follows: `http://www.rpi.edu/~djwap` - Phillip Djar being an award winning performance artist from Vancouver. (It took 45 minutes to load when I called it!) However, before we get too carried away, let us look at nested FRAMESETs.

Nested FRAMESETs

A frameset can comprise either horizontal frames (using the ROWS attribute) or vertical (using the COLS attribute). However, you can create a mixture of rows and columns using nested framesets, that is, one frameset nested (contained) within another. For example, to create the following structure, one *outer* frameset would be required and two *inner* framesets.

Frame A takes up 100% of the column in 1st row	
Frame B 30% of col in 2nd row	Frame C 70% of column in 2nd row

Each row specified by the outer frameset would require a nested frameset, each of which would describe the layout for

---

[6] But do not be surprised if this does not work on all browsers.

one of the rows. The first of the inner nests, here, describes a column taking up 100% of the first row. The second nest describes the layout for the second row, here, two columns 30% & 70% respectively.

Set up the rows first, then the columns, thus:

```
<FRAMESET ROWS= "33%, 67%">
  <FRAMESET COLS= "100%">     refers to the 33%
    <FRAME SRC ="filea.htm">

  <FRAMESET COLS= "30%, 70%">     refers to the 67%
    <FRAME = SRC= "fileb.htm">
    <FRAME = SRC= "filec.htm">
      </FRAMESET>
</FRAMESET>
```

Swapping Rows and Cols in the above frameset would result in the following structure:

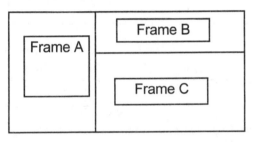

```
<FRAMESET COLS= "33%, 67%">
  <FRAMESET ROWS= "100%">
    <FRAME SRC ="filea.htm">
            do not put in an ending Frameset tag  for this inner nest!
  <FRAMESET ROWS= "30%, 70%">
    <FRAME = SRC= "fileb.htm">
    <FRAME = SRC= "filec.htm">
   </FRAMESET>               but you must do so here !
</FRAMESET>
```

Another Example

```
<FRAMESET ROWS="150, *, 130">
  <FRAMESET COLS= "100%"> .... refers to row of 150 pixels
    <FRAME  SRC ="fileA.htm">
                          no end frameset tag!
  <FRAMESET COLS= "25%, 75%"> ... refers to wildcard row

    <FRAME  SRC= "fileB.htm">
    <FRAME  SRC= "fileC.htm">

  </FRAMESET>            end frameset tag is a must !

  <FRAMESET COLS= "45%, 35%,20%">  refers to row of 130 pixels

    <FRAME  SRC= "fileD.htm">
    <FRAME  SRC= "fileE.htm">
    <FRAME  SRC= "fileF.htm">

  </FRAMESET>            end frameset tag is a must !
</FRAMESET>
```

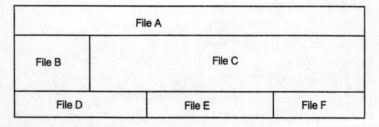

Exercise: Swap Rows for Columns in the above and work out what design you would get. With a little experimentation, you can soon work out how to use nested frames effectively. But it does take some practice.

NOTE *the correct construction for placement of the end FRAMESET tags in the above.*

When to include the </FRAMESET> tag

I could find no explanation of when to include the end FRAMESET tag in nested framesets. I read five different reference sources and only one gave any hint at all, even in those which cost £30 or more! The hint indicated that if an inner nest contains only one FRAME tag and it is the first inner nest, then do not include the </FRAMESET> tag. However, those with two or more FRAME tags in an inner nest must contain the </FRAMESET> tag. I tried various permutations but if I varied from the above, one or three frames would display, the others being ignored. I am afraid it looks as though you will have to carefully test out your code and to play around with inserting/deleting end FRAMESET tags until your desired layout is displayed. This is not very satisfactory. Somewhere out there, there may well be a full definition, but I have yet to come across it.

Why should this be? I have no idea but I suspect that those who design web browsers today come more from a graphic design background rather than a programming background. This makes for more exciting web pages, of course, but at the expense of greater laxity in defining code syntax.

Reserved target names

There are several reserved target names, each of which begins with the underscore character.

Reserved names	*This causes the targeted file to be loaded:*
_blank	into a new, blank and un-named window.
_self	into the same window or frame in which the link is contained. Useful when you wish to override targets set in the BASE tag.
_parent	into the immediate FRAMESET parent which contains this target, i.e. not the document's own frameset but the next level up. If the document has no parent, then it behaves as the _self option.
_top	into the full body of the window, replacing anything which is currently there.

Other Attributes for FRAMESET & FRAME tags

FRAMEBORDER attribute

This attribute may be placed in the FRAMESET tag or the FRAME tag. It takes the values *No* or *Yes*, the latter being the default setting. It simply turns the 3-D appearance of the frame borders on (*Yes*) or off (*No*). When it is off, the borders look flat as opposed to being in 3-D and, in addition, users will not be able to re-size the frames. This is equivalent to including the NORESIZE attribute even if it is absent.

When used in the FRAMESET tag, all frame borders are affected. When set in a FRAME tag, it applies only to that frame's borders overriding any setting in the FRAMESET tag.

```
<FRAMESET FRAMEBORDER="Yes">
<FRAME FRAMEBORDER="No">
```

Be aware that adjoining frames also have borders which are shared with other frames. You may need to adjust *all* adjacent frames to get your desired affect.

The BORDER attribute

This sets the pixel height and width (the thickness) of all frame borders and can be placed only in the outermost FRAMESET tag. It then applies to all frames in that FRAMESET and all nested FRAMESETs.

```
<FRAMESET BORDER="15">
```

Note: when a window is reduced in size to the point that there is no room to display the entire frameset in absolute pixels, the borders will always take priority.

The BORDERCOLOR attribute

This attribute may appear in the FRAMESET (to apply to all borders) and FRAME (to apply to this frame's borders) tags. It takes a *value* of a colour either as a name or an RGB hexadecimal value (Red Green Blue). Customising a colour in any Custom palette in Windows will display the decimal numbers for the colour. Convert into hexadecimal and use them in place of colour names. Very few names are recognised by all browsers, so hex is safer. See page 127 for more details.

```
<FRAMESET BORDERCOLOR="pink">
<FRAME BORDERCOLOR="FFC0CB">
```

If the FRAMEBORDER is set to "No", the BORDERCOLOR attribute will have no effect. The reason for this is that when the FRAMEBORDER attribute is turned off, the border colour will become the browser's default colour. This can be set by individual users in their browser's options.

Battle of the Browsers - An ugly scene!

Although Netscape was the first browser to introduce frames, Microsoft has produced its own version of frame tags. Most of what has been discussed so far are the same in both cases. However, some of the attributes are different.

Netscape	IE (Internet Explorer)
FRAMEBORDER uses Yes|No	same tag, but uses 0 (zero) and there is no *Yes* equivalent
BORDER	FRAMESPACING
BORDERCOLOR	BGCOLOR in <BODY> tag
MARGINWIDTH	LEFTMARGIN in <BODY> tag
MARGINHEIGHT	TOPMARGIN in <BODY> tag

To make sure your frames work on both browsers, put in *both* versions. One browser will ignore the other browser's version.

Netscape:
```
<FRAMESET ROWS="50%,50%" BORDER="10"
  FRAMEBORDER="no">
```

Internet Explorer:
```
<FRAMESET ROWS="50%,50%" FRAMESPACING="10"
  FRAMEBORDER="0">
```

A Combined effort:
```
<FRAMESET ROWS="50%,50%" BORDER="10"
  FRAMESPACING="10" FRAMEBORDER="no"
  FRAMEBORDER="0">
```

What about the <BODY> tag mentioned in the above table? And quite right to ask since it is not allowed in Netscape.

Some of IE's attributes appear in a BODY tag. This tag in a frame document will cause Netscape to fail and display a blank page. So you cannot win. Netscape does accept a <BODY> tag, if it is placed *after* the FRAMESET tag but will ignore it. However, for a BODY tag to work in IE, it must come (guess?), quite right, *before* the FRAMESET tag which upsets Netscape Navigator. So we lose again. At the time of writing, there is no way around the problem, except not to use the features unless you know that your intended audience all use the same browser. This may be the situation in an Intranet system.

Internet Explorer allows TOPMARGIN and LEFTMARGIN to be set to zero (not allowed in Netscape at the time of writing). This will allow the contents of a frame to touch the borders. But, both have to be placed in the <BODY> tag.

Miscellaneous Points

1: Tables:

<TABLE BORDER> This adds gridlines to a table.
Adding a *value* to the BORDER attribute thickens the size of a border. Thus: <TABLE BORDER=10>

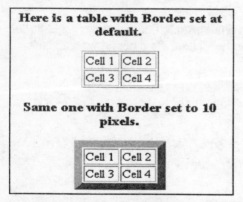

2: Cellpadding & Cellspacing

Cellspacing: This attribute allows for spacing of cells.

Cellpadding: This attribute allows for a padding (or margin) between text and cells in a table.

124

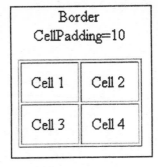

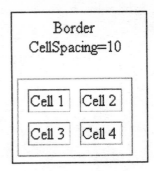

You may well need to experiment with these two to convince yourself of their difference.

```
<TABLE BORDER CELLPADDING=10>
<TABLE BORDER CELLSPACING=10>
```

3: <CENTER> tag

Note the American spelling. Almost anything can be placed in the non-empty Center tags to centre whatever they surround. They can be used to centre data in table cells, centre images, headings, etc. Although it is essentially a Netscape feature, most browsers will recognise this tag.

4: Multiple Columns - Netscape only!

```
<MULTICOL COLS=3 GUTTER=10 WIDTH=300>
```

Begin typing after this starting tag. Text will fit into the amount of space, in pixels, set by WIDTH attribute. It works like NEWSPAPER columns in word processors.

```
</MULTICOL> tag.
```

Avoid using the <PRE> tag in MUTLICOL text, since the tag overrides the normal column setting and may merge with text in adjoining columns.

It is possible to nest one multicolumn in another one.

```
<MULTICOL COLS=2 GUTTER=10 WIDTH=600>
  Type your text, etc…..
    <MULTICOL COLS=2 GUTTER=30 WIDTH=100>
```

```
      This should be a two column nested
      multicolumn.
      <IMG SRC="foxcub.gif" HEIGHT=50
         WIDTH=50>
      </MULTICOL>
  Rest of text, etc…
</MULTICOL>
```

Here is a multiple column example

At the time of writing it is a feature only of Netscape.

Here is Column 1 of the MUTLICOL feature. You simply keep typing, inserting any IMG file, headings, bulleted lists, etc. that you wish. It will behave like a newspaper column feature in word processing and will continue to snake around into the other columns. It now ends.

Best wishes.

We now continue with ordinary text which will stretch across the page..

Nested MULTICOLS

Here is a nested multiple column example

At the time of writing it is a Netscape only feature.

Here is Column 1. You simply keep typing, inserting any IMG file, headings, bulleted lists, etc. that you wish.

This is the inner nest with two columns. Again, we can include many HTML tags. One soon gets the hang of it.

This is the continuation of the outer MULTICOL column It will begin to fill up the next column and move down past the inner nested column which contains the SOAS Tree logo. However, using tables is safer and provides more control.

Best wishes.

We now continue with ordinary text which will stretch across the columns.

5: BGCOLOR & BACKGROUND attributes

These will provide a background colour or image to fill the displayed window. They are placed in the BODY tag.

The BGCOLOR tag (again, American spelling) takes either a name or hexadecimal *value*. However, only a few names are recognised by all browsers. It is safer to use a hexadecimal value based on the three basic colours: Red, Green, Blue (RGB). In Windows, it is very simple to discover the hexadecimal numbers for a particular colour. Use any application which permits you to create your own colours with the *Custom* tab of the *colour palette*. When you make your colour, you will see the decimal numbers for the RGB. Simply convert them into hexadecimal. This is easy in the scientific view of Windows calculator. Type in the decimal number and click the Hex box. The decimal numbers will be shown as hexadecimal numbers. These can then be used as the *value* for the BGCOLOR attribute.

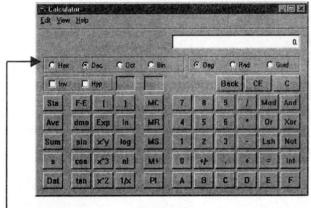

Click the Hex box after typing the decimal number.

See Appendix B for a further discussion about hexadecimal numbers.

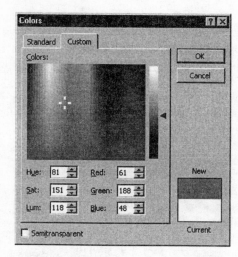

Drag the white star shape to your desired colour and read off the RGB values.

Tip: it is safer to select the colour first from the *Standard* tab and then click the *Custom* tab to read off the decimal values.

<BODY BGCOLOR="FF5609" BACKGROUND = "foxcub.gif")

The BACKGROUND attribute specifies an image file to be used to tile the background, rather like a wallpaper. Text and other images are then superimposed on this wallpaper. Yes, it is unfortunate that BGCOLOR and BACKGROUND both talk about the window background. Such is life!

If BGCOLOR and BACKGROUND attributes are both included in the *body* tag, the background will be first be coloured and then tiled with the image. The latter could cancel out the former. However, if the BACKGROUND image is transparent, the colour given by the BGCOLOR value is shown.

If you choose one of the colours from the standard set in the colour palette, you stand a better chance of getting an exact match on most browsers. A colour of your own making may not be one supported by a given computer system.

Appendix A

HTML has its origins in GML, General Markup Language, devised by IBM in the late sixties as an attempt to solve the problems of transporting documents across different computer systems. This became accepted as a *standard* by the International Standards Organisation (ISO) in Geneva, Switzerland and became known as **SGML** - ISO 8879:1986.

HTML uses a basic character set ISO 8859/1, also known as Latin-1. This uses an 8-bit alphabet. A sub-set of this, ISO 646, uses a 7-bit alphabet also known as ASCII.

Computers store characters in *bytes*, a combination of 8 bits. When you type the letter 'a', this is stored internally as a unique pattern of 8 bits (01100001 the binary equivalent of decimal 97 which is the ASCII code for letter 'a'). It is stored as a single byte. 8 bits allow for 256 (2^8) unique patterns and, therefore, 256 different characters. The first 128 characters of Latin-1 make up the ASCII character set. The remaining 128 form many of the accented and other characters commonly used in western European languages.

The ASCII set is a 7-bit pattern, still stored as a byte, but the 8th bit is not used. Why this technical summary is important is that Macintoshes and PCs running DOS do not use the Latin-1 set for their internal representation of characters. Microsoft Windows and Unix on the other hand do.

This use of different character sets can and does cause problems. Fortunately, the first 128 characters of both sets are identical and make up the ASCII set. It is the second 128 characters that are different. That is why it is always safe to use the ASCII set and, when required in an HTML document, to use *character entities* (page 39) to represent any of the non-ASCII characters.

ASCII Character Set

In the following, the first 32 of the 128 characters are special and are used to control printing and communication lines. These are not printable characters and only a few are shown. No description is given when the meaning of the character is obvious. If a character has an *entity name* this is shown in the description. The name appears between an ampersand (&) and a semi-colon (;) for example, `&quote;` Where names are not available, the ASCII code number is used preceded by a hash sign (#), thus, the tilde would be entered as a character entity as follows: `&#126;`

Note that character entity names are lowercase sensitive!

Table A.2

Number	Character	Description
0	NUL	Null character
7	Bell	rings a bell
8	BS	backspace
9	HT	horizontal tab
10	LF	line feed
13	CR	carriage return
32		space character
33	!	exclamation mark
34	"	*&quote;*
35	#	hash sign
36	$	
37	%	
38	&	ampersand - *&*
39	'	apostrophe
40	(	
41	)	
42	*	
43	+	
44	,	comma
45	-	hyphen
46	.	fullstop/period
47	/	solidus
48 - 57	0-9	digits 0 - 9
58	:	colon
59	;	semi-colon
60	<	*<*
61	=	equals
62	>	*>*

Number	Character	Description
63	?	
64	@	commercial at
65-90	Letters A - Z	uppercase letters
91	[	
92	\	backslash
93	]	
94	^	caret
95	_	underscore
96	´	acute accent
97 - 122	letters a - z	lowercase letters
123	{	left curly bracket
124			vertical bar
125	}	right curly bracket
126	~	tilde
127	DEL	delete

Note: There is no sterling (£) pound symbol in the ASCII character set. It is actually, number 163 in the Latin-1 set. That is why e-mail messages have to contain the word sterling or pounds, for example:

```
Course Fee: 200.00 pounds
```

This ensures that all readers, in particular those whose e-mail programs can cope only with ASCII, can still read the message. For the rest of the Latin-1 character set, refer to:

```
http://www.natural-innovations.com/boo/
doc-charset.html
```

References & Sources

The following references may prove useful. However, some documents can run into many pages. This can become expensive to print.

(Please note that sites come and go as do pages on the Web. The following sources were all active at the time of writing.)

Request for Comments: 1866 - the definitive standard for HTML 2.0 - the second is 77 pages in length!

```
http://www.w3.org/pub/WWW/MarkUp
```

```
ftp://ds.internic.net/rfc/rfc1866.txt
```

HTML Elements List

From Sandia National Laboratories - an excellent reference work. It includes HTML 3 and Netscape extensions.

```
http://www.sandia.gov/sci_compute/
elements.html
```

General Information about character sets on the Internet and WWW

```
http://www.echo.lu/impact/oii/chars.html
```

```
http://www.ebt.com:8080/docs/
multilingual-www.html
```

```
http://www.w3.org/hypertext/WWW/
International/Overview
```

```
http://www2.echo.lu/oii/en/
chars.html#chars
```

```
http://www.natural-innovations.com/boo/
doc-charset.html
```
(another Ithaca Web page)

Web Crawlers, Robots and Spiders

For more information about these database compilers, try:
```
http://web.nexor.co.uk/mak/doc/robots/
robots.html
```

The HTML Guru! Some highly useful questions and answers and not just for the guru.

```
http://members.aol.com/htmlguru/qanda/
index.html
```

Appendix B

Hexadecimal - Decimal Conversion

On some occasions, it may be necessary to convert a hexadecimal number to its decimal equivalent (or vice versa) in order to look up the equivalent character in the Latin-1 or some other character set. There are two methods: by use of a pocket calculator, see page 127, or as described below.

Hexadecimal

The hexadecimal number system has sixteen digits: 0 -15, whereas our decimal system has ten: 0-9 and the binary system has two: 0-1. All number systems include zero, hence 0-15 for the sixteen hexadecimal digits.

Digits 10 - 15 are given letters: A = 10, B = 11, C = 12, D = 13, E = 14 and F = 15. thus, typing D in hexadecimal refers to the equivalent decimal digit 13.

For a two-digit hex number (we do not need any more since the maximum number of characters in any set is no more than 256), convert each digit into its binary equivalent, thereby treating each digit as a group of 4 bits, thus you end up with two 4 bit groups making up a single byte - which is a group of 8 bits. We shall see why in a moment. Let us tackle the 4 bits first. From the following table, you will see that four bits, (the binary notation), allow numbers in the range 0 -15, the binary equivalent of a hexadecimal digit.

Decimal Weighting				Decimal	Hex
8	4	2	1		
0	0	0	0	0	0
0	0	0	1	1	1
0	0	1	0	2	2
0	0	1	1	3	3
0	1	0	0	4	4
0	1	0	1	5	5
0	1	1	0	6	6
0	1	1	1	7	7
1	0	0	0	8	8
1	0	0	1	9	9
1	0	1	0	10	A

1	0	1	1	11	B
1	1	0	0	12	C
1	1	0	1	13	D
1	1	1	0	14	E
1	1	1	1	15	F

To find the decimal value of B, simply add up the decimal weightings where there is a binary 1, thus: B = 8+2+1 = 11

To convert 0A to decimal, give the binary equivalent to each hex digit, thus: 0 = 0000, and A = 1010; join the two together to form an 8-bit byte, thus: 00001010.

Now enter the binary digits into the table below, and read off the decimal weightings where digit 1s appear, thus: 00100110 = 32+4+2 = 38 in decimal and 26 in hexadecimal.

Decimal Weighting								Decimal	Hex
128	64	32	16	8	4	2	1		
0	0	0	0	1	0	1	0	10	A
0	0	0	0	1	1	0	1	13	D
0	0	1	0	0	1	1	0	38	26
0	1	1	0	1	0	1	1	107	6B
1	0	0	0	1	1	1	1	143	8F
1	1	0	0	1	1	1	0	206	CE
0	0	1	1	1	0	0	0		
1	0	0	0	0	0	0	1		
1	1	1	1	1	1	1	1		

Try the last three for yourself, the answers are given in the footnote.[2]

To convert from decimal to hexadecimal, convert the decimal to an 8-bit binary number, according to the decimal weightings for the above table. Then split the eight bits into two groups of four, and give each group its equivalent hex value as shown in the first table.

Thus: 100 in decimal = 64+32+4 = 0110 0100 in binary or 64 in hexadecimal.

---

[2] 00111000 = 56 Dec & 38 Hex;
10000001 = 129 Dec & 81 Hex
11111111 = 255 Dec & FF Hex.

Glossary

ASCII
American Standard Code for Information Interchange. A code for representing characters and which is supported by almost all computer manufacturers.

attribute
in HTML, it further defines the use of a tag or element.

browsers
programs used to find and display information on the World Wide Web, WWW, using hypertext.

character entity
method used in HTML whereby ASCII and non-ASCII characters can be inserted into HTML documents.

client
a program which extracts a service or information on your behalf from a server computer somewhere on a network.

element
term for the HTML markup codes.

empty tag
has no associated end tag.

ftp
file transfer protocol - a standard method of transferring files between, often, distant sites.

gateway program
a program written to process data sent from a Web form document.

GML
General Markup Language devised by IBM in the 1960s.

gopher
an early menu type system for searching for information on the Internet.

home page   the default page you see each time you
call up your WWW browser. You can
choose to make your own home page or
use someone else's. Each site creates its
own home page.

host   a computer on a network which allows
remote users to access its facilities.

HTML   the hypertext markup language
recognised by Web browser telling them
how to display Web pages.

HTML+   refers to version 3 of HTML.

http   the Hyper-Text Transfer Protocol is used
extensively by WWW to transfer
information between networks.

hypertext   text or images which contain a link to
where further information about the
phrase or picture is stored. By clicking on
a piece of hypertext, a new page of
information pops up.

hypertext-link   the link address to where information is
stored when a hypertext phrase is
clicked.

IAB   Internet Architecture Board, a group
which makes decisions about Internet
standards and other important matters.

IETF   Internet Engineering Task Force, a
voluntary group which investigates
technical problems and reports back to
the IAB.

IP   Internet Protocol, the rules which the
many different operating systems use to

communicate with each other over the Internet.

LAN Local Area Network, a collection of computers which can communicate with each other in a local vicinity such as a building or university campus.

markup publishing term meaning how the human printer has to format text and pictures in a book.

monospace font typeface where each character is given exactly the same amount of space.

non-empty tag has both a start and an end tag.

packet data transmitted over the Internet is broken into smaller packets by TCP, usually about 1500 characters. They have to be re-assembled at the other end.

partial address same as relative address or link.

platform frequently refers to the type of operating system being used on a computer.

point size printer's term for measuring character size. There are 72 points to an inch.

proportional font typeface whereby each character is given the amount of space depending on its shape and width.

protocol standards or rules which define how information is transmitted between computers.

relative links	a hypertext address relative to the address of the current document.
RFC 1866	Requests For Comments 1866 which defines HTML 2.0.
server	software which allows one computer to offer a service to another computer. Client software on the other computer, requests the service from the server. Sometimes, the computer with the server software is also called the server.
SGML	the Standard General Markup Language.
site	the location of the network where WWW and other documents and/or images are held.
tag	term for the HTML markup codes.
TCP	Transmission Control Protocol, the system by which information is divided into packets for transmission over the Internet.
telnet	a simple protocol which allows you to login to a remote network.
text formatter	pre-dates word processors where both the markup codes and the actual text had to be typed in by the author.
URL	Uniform (or Universal) Resource Locator. The method of specifying the location of resources on the Internet. Used mainly with WWW.
WAN	Wide Area Network. A network which may be national or global in extent, as

opposed to a local area network.

Web browser   one of the many programs which are able to retrieve and display information over the WWW.

Web Master   someone who maintains and mounts information on the Web for an organisation's LAN.

Web page   a screen display of a document found on the WWW.

white space   printer's term referring to any form of spacing, such as tabs, normal spaces, extra spacing between words, etc.

WWW   World Wide Web.

Index